ENJOY GUIDED RE

CW01497062

Teacher Book with Copymasters

Key Stage 1: Level 2A>3

Julie Galliard/ Roger Hurn

For the novels:

- *Mark Spark in the Dark* by Jacqueline Wilson
- *Cool as a Cucumber* by Michael Morpurgo
- *The Finger Eater* by Dick King-Smith
- *Harry the Poisonous Centipede* by Lynn Reid Banks
- *The Pea and the Princess* by Mini Grey
- *Winnie's New Computer* by Korky Paul & Valerie Thomas
- *The Enormous Crocodile* by Roald Dahl
- *Dinosaur School* by Dick-King Smith
- *Pup on the Pitch* by Sophie Smiley
- *Horrid Henry's Underpants* by Francesca Simon

(APP Reading Links can be found after the last section)

Badger
LEARNING

INTRODUCTION TO GUIDED READING

Learning Objectives

These relate to the Primary Framework for Literacy, the objectives for Reading at Year Level 2A>3 and the Assessing Pupils Progress (APP) Reading and Writing Assessment focuses.

- Explain and comment on writers' use of language, including grammatical and literary features at word and sentence level.
- Read short stories and serialised longer stories and review the main features of the characters, plot and setting. Discuss views, response and preferences as a class. Compare settings and analyse words and phrases used for description.

Reading Assessment Guidelines, Levels 1-5

AF1 - use a range of strategies, including accurate decoding of text, to read for meaning.

AF2 - understand, describe, select or retrieve information, events or ideas from texts and use quotation and reference to text.

AF3 - deduce, infer or interpret information, events or ideas from texts.

AF4 - identify and comment on the structure and organisation of texts, including grammatical and presentational features at text level.

AF5 - explain and comment on writers' use of language, including grammatical and literary features at word and sentence level.

AF6 - identify and comment on writers' purposes and viewpoints, and the overall effect of the text on the reader.

AF7 - relate texts to their social, cultural and historical traditions.

Writing Assessment Guidelines, Levels 1-5

AF1 - write imaginative, interesting and thoughtful texts.

AF2 - produce texts which are appropriate to task, reader and purpose.

AF3 - organise and present whole texts effectively, sequencing and structuring information, ideas and events.

AF4 - construct paragraphs and use cohesion within and between paragraphs.

AF5 - vary sentences for clarity, purpose and effect.

AF6 - write with technical accuracy of syntax and punctuation in phrases, clauses and sentences.

AF7 - select appropriate and effective vocabulary.

AF8 - use correct spelling.

Criteria for selecting titles

The books are all fiction – picture books that include popular titles by well-established authors familiar to most KS1 teachers. They have been selected after consultation with Literacy Subject Leaders and Key Stage 1 class teachers. The reading level of each book is given at the start of the relevant section. The intention is to help children to engage with titles that they will enjoy and want to read and re-read, while supporting them to acquire the important skills of decoding and early comprehension.

Titles

There are ten titles levelled at either 2A>3. Each title has the following accompanying guidance:

- A story synopsis
- Main teaching objectives
- Notes and ideas for two guided reading sessions
- A series of follow-on activities
- Suggestions for writing opportunities

Story synopsis

This section summarises the story, thus familiarising teachers with unknown texts.

Main teaching objectives

Reading objectives for each title relate to the reading strand of the Core Areas of Learning as identified in the Primary National Strategy Renewed Framework for Literacy:

- Word reading skills and strategies
- Understand and interpret texts
- Engage with and respond to texts
- The objectives have been linked to the QCA Assessment Focuses for Reading. They are referred to throughout the two reading sessions.

Guided Reading Sessions

The two guided reading sessions are broken down as follows:

- Book introduction
- Return to text
- Strategy check
- Response to text-
- Independent reading
- Next steps

Book introduction

This section suggests ways in which the text can be introduced, for example, through discussing the front cover and title, reading the blurb or the first part of the book prior to the first session and using this knowledge to discuss and predict the content.

Strategy check

In this section reference is made to the following:

- Discriminating and blending phonemes as a strategy for reading unknown words.
- Using knowledge of syntax, context, word origin and structure to support decoding and establish meaning.
- Specific features of the text, such as the way the author has used punctuation, to encourage expressive reading.
- New and unfamiliar vocabulary the children will meet in the text.

Independent reading

The children are given a reading focus and asked to read independently. For this part of the session, they will sometimes be required to record on Post-it notes or on whiteboards. While each child reads their own book, the teacher or other adult works with one child and then another, asking each one to read aloud from where they are up to, prompting children to apply phonic strategies and to read for meaning.

Return to the text

Follow-up questions are provided to encourage discussion which is sometimes related to the independent reading task.

Response to text

This section is most important as it allows children to respond imaginatively and evaluate the stories. Different types of questions have been suggested; they encourage children to read between and beyond the lines, as well as helping them to develop a personal response to the stories to encourage thinking about the overall effect of the book on the reader. Some general questions related to children's independent reading outside the sessions are provided.

Next steps

Follow-on activities are provided, although they may not always be required. They contain materials that teachers can use and adapt to suit the needs of their children. They can be introduced and explained at the end of the reading session. Some children may need the support of another adult to work on their activities to allow them to interact with the text and make comprehension work meaningful and engaging. The activities can be done on the sheets or used in reading journals; pairs or groups of children can work together on some of them. They are especially useful as independent tasks during reading sessions. Most can be adapted to suit other books.

These guided reading sessions and follow-up materials are intended to provide ideas and suggestions for working with these texts in order to meet key reading objectives. Many teachers will use them as starting points for developing their own guided reading plans. In this way it is hoped that both teacher and pupil will come to enjoy Guided Reading.

Best of luck,

Julie Galliard

Mark Spark in the Dark *Jacqueline Wilson*
Level 2A>3

Two stories in one book that can be used together or separately. It will be necessary to read them in the order they appear in the book for the second guided session to follow on and cover the same objectives as the first session.

SUMMARY OF "MARK SPARK" PP.1-40

We are introduced to Mark Spencer, known as Mark Spark, when Miss Moss, his class teacher, is talking about Guide Dogs for the Blind. Mark gets very excited because his Great Gran, with whom he spends a lot of time when his parents are at work, is nearly blind. The class make suggestions for raising money to train a guide dog.

Mark assumes his Great Gran will have the guide dog and he can help to train it. He is bitterly disappointed when she tells him she is too old for a guide dog, but feels better after watching Neighbours and reading aloud to Great Gran from her favourite book, Love's Flame.

Miss Moss organises a Bring and Buy sale to raise money for the dog. Great Gran knits some socks for Mark to take. They are strange shapes and colours but Mark defends them loyally when the other children laugh at them. He buys them and wears them for the next fund-raising event – a sponsored walk. Not being very energetic, Mark is soon left behind. He stops to 'air' his feet and finds a toe poking out of one of the socks. He thinks it looks like a nose, so he makes it sneeze. He likes 'playing socks'.

The next fund raising event is a class concert. Mark is stuck for ideas so Great Gran suggests he acts out her favourite book, Love's Flame, with puppets. The puppets are made from the socks and Mark Spark's talent for speaking in different voices ensures the show is a great success. He continues to do puppet shows in the playground and charges his friends one penny to watch to raise more money for the guide dog. Eventually the school raises enough money to train a guide dog; when the photo arrives, the dog is called Mark.

SUMMARY OF "MARK SPARK IN THE DARK" PP.43-82

Mark and his friends are walking home from school; Mark is jumping in puddles and making his new trainers very muddy. Louise tells the boys she is getting new trainers and a pink tent for her birthday and, as a birthday treat, she invites Jason and Mark to sleep overnight in it. Mark has a real problem with this.

Mark's secret problem is a fear of the dark. He knows he will not be able to sleep outside in a tent but cannot tell his friends. Great Gran guesses there is something wrong and eventually Mark confides in her. She promises to sort something out.

Mark tells his friends he is unable to spend the night in the tent because he has to stay with Great Gran, who is afraid of the dark and burglars. Louise invites Lily to stay in the tent and Mark has to listen to the three children planning the birthday treat. He is especially sorry to miss the camp stove feast – sausages and pancakes.

Great Gran provides a 'camp fire feast' around the electric fire in her lounge, and Mark snuggles up happily in bed, feeling very full and secure in the knowledge that Great Gran is beside him. When he wakes up in the night, following a strange dream, Great Gran is missing and he hears her voice wailing from the garden. After hearing further thumps and bangs, Mark thinks Great Gran is being hurt and hurtles out of bed and out into the dark garden to protect her. He bumps into Great Gran, who tells him it was only a cat. She is impressed at his bravery and Mark discovers that the dark is not so frightening after all.

GUIDED READING – MARK SPARK IN THE DARK

APP Reading Links

Assessment Focus

AF1 - Session 1: Level 2/3
       Session 2: Level 2/3
AF2 - Session 1: Level 2/3
       Session 2: Level 2/3
AF3 - Session 1: Level 2/3
       Session 2: Level 3
AF4 - Session 2: Level 2/3
AF6 - Session 2: Level 2/3

Session 1 (AF1, AF2, AF3)

Book introduction
Use the cover of the book to make some predictions about Mark Spark. Record these on a whiteboard or flipchart to use later. Ask questions about his appearance and what they can infer from his expression and the background of the picture.

Ask the children if they have ever felt afraid of the dark. When and why? How did they overcome it? Explain that there are two stories in this book about the character Mark Spark. See the contents page and blurb.

Strategy check
Check children's understanding of all four reading strategies (searchlights). Demonstrate their use if necessary. Tell the children another way of working out longer words is to break them up into chunks or syllables, then blend the chunks together into the whole word. Demonstrate with im-it-at-ing from page 4 and mur-mur-ing from page 36. Listen to see if the word sounds right. Check their meanings. Show children two more words: sponsored page 8 and endearments page 36. Ask them to break the words into their syllables in order to read them.

Use whiteboards. Check children understand the meanings of these words by reading the whole sentences from the text and demonstrating how to re-run the sentence while listening for sense and predicting the meaning using grammar and context.

Independent reading
Tell children the focus for reading is to identify the main characters in the text, how they behave, what they feel and how we know. Give out CM1 so children can begin to record their findings if they finish reading. Ask children to begin reading at Chapter 1 silently, or very quietly to themselves. Listen to each child in turn read aloud, noting and supporting the use of the strategies outlined above. Ask children to stop reading at the end of the first story (p.40).

Return to the text
Praise the children's reading and use of strategies as demonstrated. You could use the following words as examples: *tartan* (p.1); *labrador* (p.5); *original* (p.9); *practical* (p.9); *wincing* (p.11); *disappointed* (p.17); *brilliant* (p.22); *performance* (p.37) and *eventually* (p.39).

Response to text
Ask children to share what they have found out about Mark in this first story and encourage them to find evidence in the text for their views. Ask the children how they thought Mark felt at the end of the story. How would they feel to have a guide dog named after them?

Characteristics and feelings to identify include: greed (pp.2, 13, 14, 30); love of animals (p.2); sense of unfairness (p.4 *slumped in his seat*); excitable and noisy (pp.6, 8, 9, 11); cares about Great Gran and is kind to her (p.16 when he is disappointed she won't be having a dog, p.18 reads to her); good reader – able to dramatise characters (pp.18, 34-36); loyal to Great Gran and to friends (pp.21-25); not energetic (pp.26-27); full of bright ideas throughout the story.

Next steps
Demonstrate how to complete the chart on CM1, adding characteristics and evidence. Ask children to complete reading the story and fill in the chart before the next reading session.

Session 2 (AF1, AF2, AF3, AF4, AF6)

Introduction
Talk about the character of Mark. Ask each child to give an opinion of him, supported with evidence from the text already read. Model a response of your own first. E.g. *I think Mark is a good friend because he used his last 5p to buy Louise's mum's knitted toilet roll cover at the Bring and Buy sale so she didn't have to take it home again.*

Strategy check
Identify how the writer has suggested some of Mark's feelings through the use of dialogue, the way it is punctuated and by the use of adverbs. Refer to the conversation on page 47 when Jason is replying to Louise, Louise's reaction to the worm on page 48, the way Mark would have spoken on page 50 (sadly) and on page 51 (sighing). Ask the children to read some of these passages with expression, taking account of both punctuation and adverbs. Notice how the author has used punctuation to exaggerate the problem on page 52. Pages 60-61 are also useful to demonstrate Mark's hesitant, worried tone and Great Gran's comforting and supportive words.

Independent reading
Remind children of the plot of the previous story. Mark has a problem, his friends are involved, he has various ideas but it is Great Gran who supports him and works out a solution to his problem. Ask the children to identify the problem in this story as they read, and identify Great Gran's way of solving it without Mark losing face. Listen to the children read, encouraging them to use expression to make the text interesting for the listener.

Return to the text

Ask the children to select a short piece of dialogue that they particularly enjoyed reading and ask them to read it aloud with the appropriate expression. Put the sentence into context before reading. Praise each child's reading.

Response to text

Ask the children to outline the events in this story, focusing particularly on the build up, problem, climax and resolution. Ask key questions such as why did the problem arise, what was the problem, who helped to solve it and how, what was the result? Do the children think Great Gran ventured into the garden at night on purpose? Was there really a cat? Have they ever been afraid of the dark? When? How did they overcome it or are they still frightened? Value all the different opinions expressed here.

Next steps

Fill in CM2 to show how events are linked in stories. As part of a whole class plenary, ask a child from the guided reading group to use CM2 to tell the story to the class. Select two of the other children to be in the hot seat as Mark and Great Gran and use the question cards on CM3 and CM4 for members of the class to ask questions of them. Ensure all children who have studied the Mark Spark stories have a turn. This is a useful activity to support speaking and listening, the development of questioning skills and to promote the stories to other members of the class.

Writing opportunities

- Write an account of a day in the life of Mark Spencer in the form of a diary.
- Write an imaginary letter to the Guide Dogs for the Blind Association telling them what Miss Moss' class did to raise money for training a guide dog.
- Investigate other jobs that dogs are trained to do for humans. (Hearing dogs, sniffer dogs used at earthquake sites, mountain rescue dogs could all be included.) Create a short fact file about each one.
- Write another adventure for Mark Spark, Louise and Jason.
- Re-write one of these stories as a short play. It could be practised and performed as part of a school Assembly.
- Create the report card Miss Moss might write about Mark at the end of the school year.
- Make a list of the things you think Mark Spark might have in his bedroom.

Name . . . . Date . . . .

All about Mark

Put a smiley face in the column you most agree with.
Write a comment to justify your opinion.

Characteristic	Yes	No	Evidence
kind	☺		He uses the last of his money to buy the toilet roll cover that Louise's mum has made when it is left on the stall at the end of the Bring and Buy sale because he can see his friend is getting upset.
brave			
greedy			
clever			
unhappy			

Name . . . . Date. . . . .

Story plan

The characters in this story are:

The event they are planning is:

The problem is:

Great Gran solves the problem by:

At the end, Mark feels:

1 Mark Spark in the Dark (3)

Questions to ask Mark

Cut out and laminate these cards and give to members of the class to ask 'Mark' when he is in the hot seat. The questions can relate to either story. A question mark means you have to think of your own question.

When did you feel really proud of yourself? Why did you feel like this?	What was it like to perform in the concert with the sock puppets?	?
How did you feel when your friends were planning the birthday celebrations? Why?	?	Describe how you felt when you woke up in the night and heard Gran wailing outside in the dark.
What do you think of your Great Gran? How does she help to look after you?	Do you like being in Miss Moss' class? What are your favourite subjects?	Who are your best friends? Say what you like about them.

Mark Spark in the Dark (4)

Questions to ask Great Gran

Cut out and laminate these cards and give to members of the class to ask 'Great Gran' when she is in the hot seat.
The questions can relate to either story. A question mark means you have to think of your own question.

Do you look forward to the time when Mark comes to your house after school? Why?

What do you like most about Mark?

What do you like doing when you are not cooking for Mark?

What did you think of the present Mark bought you from the Bring and Buy stall?

?

?

How did you know there was something worrying Mark when he came in from school with muddy trainers?

What was your idea to help Mark with his problem about the dark?

How did you know there was a cat in the garden in the middle of the night? Was there really a cat?

Cool as a Cucumber *by Michael Morpurgo*
Level 2A>3

SUMMARY OF THE STORY

Mrs Mapleton, a teacher at St Peter's School, decides her class will create a vegetable garden to celebrate the Queen's Jubilee. She promises the hardest worker will receive the first cucumber.

Peter likes cucumbers so he digs enthusiastically. Soon, he starts to find interesting objects – worms, sandals, beetles and an old coin. Hoping to find more valuable treasures, Peter continues to dig during playtime.

Peter unearths a large, cucumber-shaped bomb. None of the teachers believe him when he rushes to the staff room to report the find so he takes matters into his own hands and calls the emergency services – all of them. Peter becomes a hero. He feels important when interviewed by the news reporters; he appears on the front page of the local newspaper and the television.

The bomb is exploded safely, and the resulting crater used to grow vegetables, some of which are taken by the children to London, along with a card showing photos of the garden, to give to the Queen. A guard receives them and the children subsequently receive a letter from the Queen thanking them for the vegetables, particularly the cucumber from which the Queen's sandwiches have been made.

GUIDED READING – COOL AS A CUCUMBER

APP Reading Links

Assessment Focus

AF1 - Session 1: Level 2/3
Session 2: Level 2/3
AF3 - Session 1: Level 2/3
Session 2: Level 2/3
AF5 - Session 1: Level 2/3
Session 2: Level 2/3

2

Session 1 (AF1, AF3, AF5)

Book introduction
Discuss the cover of the book. Identify the main character and setting. Discuss possible meanings of cool; explain simile. Ask the children to talk to a partner about the character on the cover. What can they tell you about him? Ask for reasons. Listen to some ideas. These could be recorded on a whiteboard. Read the blurb to the children, demonstrating how to read with expression and take account of the punctuation. Add information about the character – name, not keen on digging. Why do they think Peter is not keen on digging?

Strategy check
Show some verb cards from the story – *wracking* (p.11); *ignored* (p.12); *worried* (p.13); *digging* (p.14); *urging* (p.14); *discovered* (p.17); *laughed* (p.20); *tinkling* (p.23); *plunged* (p.26); *scraped* (p.26). What do they notice about the endings? Discuss verb tenses. Remind children of the searchlights and encourage them to read the words. Discuss meanings by reading the sentence from the text containing the verb and asking children for ideas.

Independent reading
Remind children of the objectives and ask them to read to the end of Chapter 2 independently with the following questions in mind. What is Mrs Mapleton like? How do we know? How does she behave? What does Peter feel about her? Do you like her? While the children are reading, listen to each one read a few sentences aloud and check that reading strategies (searchlights) are being applied to unfamiliar words.

Return to the text
Praise children's use of reading strategies and correct reading of verbs. Ask them to give their opinions of Mrs Mapleton, locating words, phrases and examples of behaviour in the text to support their views. Would they like to be in Mrs Mapleton's class? Give reasons.

Response to text
Refer children to pages 26 and 27. How has the author begun to create suspense here? Guide children to the repetition of very, use of the phrase whatever it was to make the reader think of possibilities, construction of the sentence beginning with And it wasn't… and the comparative adjectives *bigger, rounder, longer*. How has the author built up more suspense on page 28?

Use of the word massive, description of the shape, use of simile. Note adjectives on page 29 and Peter's reaction on page 30. Ask children how they would have reacted and why.

Next steps
Ask children to read to the end of Chapter 4 independently, noting any words they find difficult and extending their views on the main characters. Use CM1, CM2 and CM3.

Session 2 (AF1, AF3, AF5)

Introduction
Recap on events to the end of Chapter 3. Ask children to outline the main events. Direct them to page 31. Read aloud, emphasising the action verbs. They are used to create excitement and build up the drama of the find. In subsequent pages, note how Peter's words contrast with the comments and reactions of the teachers. Ask the children to read Peter's words aloud, stressing the urgency and rising panic he is feeling. How would you have felt when Mrs Mapleton didn't believe you?

What other ways does the author build up the tension? Include illustrations on pages 37-41, quick passing of time, speed of events and verbs expressing noises that we relate to emergencies (p.37-39) and the use of short, repetitious sentences on page 41, leading to silence.

Briefly recap on events in Chapter 4; ensure children have recorded Peter's reactions on CM3. Draw attention to page 47 and Peter's words to the reporter. Make links to the title of the book. Ask the children what they would have said in reply to the reporter's question. If time, children could role-play the interview between the reporter and Peter.

Strategy check
Ask children to look at CM1 – new words and phrases. Locate their position in the text. Discuss meanings and strategies for reading and understanding them. Ensure children refer to re-running the sentence to listen for sense, and reading on to the end to see if they can work out the word and its meaning.

Independent reading

Ask children to read to the end of the book silently, filling in CM2 and CM3 as they finish. Listen to individual children reading aloud, praise their use of the searchlights and particularly their use of the strategies described above.

Return to the text

Ask children for their opinions of the main characters. Refer to CM2 and CM3. Children find references to the characters in the text and read aloud the sections that provide evidence for their views. Value all responses and be prepared for differing views.

Response to text

What do the children think Peter felt about Mrs Mapleton at the beginning of the book, when she introduced the idea of a vegetable garden, in the middle of the book, when she wouldn't believe what he had found, and at the end, when she cried? Find words and phrases that the author uses to suggest how Peter and the others feel about their teacher.

Next steps

Use CM4 for a word sort. Identify the different rules for adding -ed to verbs to create the past tense. List these on a chart to present to the rest of the class in a plenary session or as part of the whole class spelling work. Encourage the children to read other books by Michael Morpurgo and create a class book of reviews and author information.

Writing opportunities

- Create the front page of the newspaper that reported the finding of the bomb.
- Design the card the children made to take to the Queen. Refer to page 54 for details of the contents.
- Write a note to pupils who will be in Mrs Mapleton's class next year, telling them what to expect.
- Make a safety poster saying what to do if you find a dangerous object.
- Draw and label some ideas for using cucumbers – e.g. cucumber sandwiches, salads.
- Make a set of instructions for growing vegetables.

2 Cool as a Cucumber

Verb cards for 'Strategy check' – Session 1

wracking	ignored
worried	digging
urging	discovered
laughed	tinkling
plunged	scraped

2 Cool as a Cucumber (1)

Name . . . . Date. . . . .

My list of new words

When you find new words that you do not know, or have difficulty reading, write the page number and the word.
Use a dictionary to help you to find the meaning of the word.

Page	Word or phrase	Meaning
31	hared	raced or ran very fast

2 Cool as a Cucumber (1)

Name . . . . Date. . . . .

My list of new words

When you find new words that you do not know, or have difficulty reading, write the page number and the word.
Use a dictionary to help you to find the meaning of the word.

Page	Word or phrase	Meaning
31	hared	raced or ran very fast

2 Cool as a Cucumber (2)

Name . . . . Date . . . .

All About Mrs Mapleton

Record your thoughts and opinions about Mrs Mapleton.

Page number	Words and phrases used to describe Mrs Mapleton	What I know or think about Mrs Mapleton

Name . . . . Date. . . . .

All About Peter

Record your thoughts and opinions about Peter.

Page number	What Peter does or says	What I think about Peter

2 Cool as a Cucumber (4)

Name . . . . Date. . . . .

Verbs from Cool as a Cucumber

Copy and laminate this sheet for each pair of children. Cut them out so each card has both present and past tense on it (18 cards in all). Ask the children to sort the cards and create spelling rules for adding -ed endings. Check these in a plenary.

gawp	gawped	cry	cried
worry	worried	discover	discovered
laugh	laughed	decide	decided
stamp	stamped	bury	buried
wonder	wondered	crash	crashed
drop	dropped	gape	gaped
wait	waited	wave	waved
stop	stopped	dial	dialled
sign	signed	allow	allowed

The Finger Eater *by Dick King-Smith*
Level 2A>3

SUMMARY OF THE STORY

This is a story with all the elements of a traditional tale. In the cold lands of the north lives Ulf, a troll who likes to eat fingers. He fools his victims by pretending to be polite and well-mannered and offering to shake hands. As soon as he grasps the strangers' hands, he bites off the fingers and runs off as fast as his bow-legs can carry him. Many of the local villagers have one finger missing, including the children.

Gudrun lives with her parents, who both lost a finger to Ulf when they were children. She is warned about the troll by her parents but resolves to do something to stop him eating fingers. Not long after, she meets Ulf but he fails to trick her and she bravely stands her ground, telling him that eating fingers is wrong. She even throws milk in his face before scurrying home to think long and hard about how she can make him give up his horrid habit.

Suddenly Gudrun has a brilliant idea. She notices a discarded reindeer antler that resembles a hand. She covers it with a glove made of strong reindeer hide and walks off to meet the troll with her new hand outstretched in greeting.

Ulf cannot believe his luck and grabs Gudrun's right hand, shoves it into his mouth and bites as hard as he can. Every razor sharp tooth in his mouth is shattered and smashed while his agonising cry circles round the mountains. He begs Gudrun to help him, which she does by using some giant pliers to remove the broken teeth from his mouth.

Ulf's mouth recovers but he does not totally lose his bad habit. Hill folk cannot grow new teeth, however, so when he catches hands in the future there is only the pressure of toothless gums. Eventually he disappears back to his hole, sulking, and the tale of how Gudrun put paid to the wicked ways of Ulf, the Finger-eater, passes into legend.

3

GUIDED READING – THE FINGER EATER

APP Reading Links

Assessment Focus

AF1	-	Session 1: Level 2/3
		Session 2: Level 2/3
AF2	-	Session 1: Level 2/3
		Session 2: Level 2/3
AF3	-	Session 1: Level 2
		Session 2: Level 3
AF4	-	Session 2: Level 2/3
AF7	-	Session 1: Level 2/3
		Session 2: Level 2/3

Session 1 (AF1, AF2, AF3, AF7)

Book introduction

Talk about the cover of the book. Use the blurb for an overview of the story. What is a troll? Where have they heard of one before? What happened to him and why? What type of story is the Billy Goats Gruff? Ask the children what type of story we might expect here? What else supports the view that it is a book written in the traditional tale genre. Use the picture of Gudrun on the back cover to support the discussion. Talk about her appearance and expression. Why might she be smiling?

Strategy check

Ask the children to tell you the strategies they use to work out unfamiliar words. Ensure all four searchlights are covered. Ask children to apply searchlights to some of these words from the story – *unusual* (p.9); *spied* (p.12); *politely* (p.12); *tolerant* (p.19); *considered* (p.20). Check both decoding and meaning by referring children to the sentences where the words appear. Check knowledge of long vowel digraphs – *ie, i-e, er*.

Independent reading

Refer children to the picture at the start of the story on page 9 and ask them to suggest the setting of the story from the picture. One focus for reading is to use clues in the text and pictures to work out the setting and the second is to find out how Ulf tricked his victims. Ask all the children to read silently. Finish the independent reading at the end of Chapter 3 (p.46) if possible.

Listen to each child read a short section aloud, support them to use the strategies already described and help them to identify unknown meanings.

Return to the text

Where do the children think the story is set? What are the clues? Does it resemble a real place? How? What evidence is there that this is an imaginary place? Draw attention to characters, costumes, homes and way of life. Ask children to describe briefly how Ulf tricked his victims. Check children understand *index finger* and the meaning of the two idioms on page 20. Look at page 29 and apply reading strategies to the word resolute. What do the children think it means? How can they work it out?

Response to text

Ask the children how the pictures contribute to their understanding and enjoyment of the story. Pages 14-17, 40-45 are useful for this. Allow children to choose a picture and give their own reasons for choosing it. Encourage them to note details in the pictures – expressions, speech and thought bubbles. Demonstrate how pictures and the text work together to create humour and support the reader's understanding.

Next steps

Use CM1 to create a wanted poster for Ulf the Troll. Begin to fill in CM2, to list the details of the story. Ensure all members of the group have read to the end of Chapter 3 (p.46) before the next session.

Session 2 (AF1, AF2, AF3, AF4, AF7)

Introduction

What clues were there in the first three chapters to identify the genre of this story? Identify opening words, characters, good versus bad and their appearance – focus particularly on Gudrun's cornflower blue eyes and golden hair (p.22) – inclusion of country setting and animals. Ask pairs of children to act out a meeting between Ulf and a stranger to show they have understood how Ulf tricked his victims. Recap on the content of the story so far. Ensure the children identify Gudrun's determination to stop Ulf's nasty habit. Ask for ideas as to what she might do next.

3

Strategy check

Ask children to identify what strategies (searchlights) they use when reading. Apply these to words which may be unfamiliar such as *resembling* (p.50); *protruded* (p.50); *emerged* (p.51); *approaching* (p.51); *concealed* (p.54); *revealed* (p.54). Assess children's knowledge of vowel digraphs – *er, oa, ea*. Read words in context and support children to work out the meanings.

Independent reading

Ask children to read to the end of the book and identify how Gudrun finally put paid to Ulf's wicked ways. Ask them to continue to notice how the illustrations and the text work together to create humour and help the reader to understand the text.

Listen to each child read a section of text and check that the strategies outlined above are being applied. Praise children's efforts.

Return to the text

Praise children's use of searchlights and ask one or two to demonstrate how they applied them to their reading. How did Gudrun finally stop Ulf from eating fingers? How do you think Ulf felt when he bit the reindeer's antler? What would he have thought when he saw Gudrun approaching him with the pliers? (p.56) What do you feel about Ulf at the end of the story? Have your feelings for him changed during the story? How? Some children might sympathise with Ulf because people laugh at him and he disappears down into his hole alone. Ask them to justify their feelings using evidence from the text and pictures.

Return to the blurb and ask children to explain the significance of the words bites off more than he can chew and plucky.

Response to text

What further evidence is there that this is in the style of a traditional tale. Note good triumphs over evil and the final page. Ask children to work in pairs to tell each other which part of the text they liked best and to give their reasons. Listen in and take some feedback. How is this story different from some other traditional tales they have read? Which did they like best and why?

Next steps

Complete CM2. Use the information to support a talk about the book to the group or class. Use CM3 to create an advertisement for the book. Ask the children to create a publicity poster to make other children buy this book. What would they want to tell them about it?

Use CM4 to make a poster for the children who live in the Cold Lands of the North to tell them what to do to keep safe when they see the Troll. Tell the children to base their advice on the text, e.g. Don't shake hands with the Troll.

Writing opportunities

- Re-write a section of the book as a play. Good sections would be Ulf's meeting with a stranger, the conversation between Gudrun and her parents when she first hears about the troll, or either of the encounters between Gudrun and Ulf.
- Write some rules for keeping safe that the parents who live in the Cold Lands of the North might have given to their children. Use some of the speech bubbles to help you.
- Write a paragraph to say what happens to Ulf after he disappears into his hole in the hill.
- Create a newspaper report with a headline relating to Ulf and his terrible habit.
- Make a model of the setting for the story out of cardboard, small world figures, Plasticene and other junk items. Label the various parts that featured in the story – e.g. the village, with the school, Gudrun's camp, the meadow where the reindeer graze and Ulf's hole in the hill. Use the pictures and the text to add details such as the distant mountains, the flowers (p.35) and the cooking pot over the fire (p.24). Each child in the group could write a short paragraph saying what happened at each of the labelled places. These could then be displayed next to the model in the correct sequence for other children to read.
- An alternative way of using the model would be to create another adventure for Gudrun using the same setting. Ensure the children talk their ideas through before writing the story and show them how to use story planning frames to structure their narratives.

Name . . . . Date. . . . .

Wanted

ULF
the troll

AGE:

ADDRESS:

DESCRIPTION:

WANTED FOR:

Name . . . . Date . . . .

Story grammar

Title:

Author: **Publisher:**

Characters

Setting

Plot

Themes

Name . . . . Date . . . .

The Finger Eater

Name . . . . Date . . . .

BE SAFE

Do

Do

Don't

Don't

Harry the Poisonous Centipede
by Lynne Reid Banks Level 3

SUMMARY OF THE STORY

Harry, a poisonous centipede, lives in a series of underground tunnels with his mother, Belinda, who, being very protective, warns him of the dangers of the No-top-world – where snakes, birds and humans live. She shows him the forbidden tunnel and the pool from where the Up-Pipe leads to the Place of the Hoo-Mins. Unknown to Belinda, Harry revisits the pool and almost drowns.

George, a young centipede who lives and hunts alone, is Harry's best friend. He teases Harry for still living with his mother and leads him into all sorts of scrapes, such as the visit to the No-top-world where a mole-cricket threatens to attack them. Harry just manages to save them by giving it a poisonous bite.

George and Harry plan an adventure underground when George dares Harry to show him the Up-Pipe. The two attempt to climb the drain, but are washed out by a sudden rush of water and Harry finally learns to swim, saving his friend as they are swept along by the current. George believes the Hoo-Mins sent the water deliberately and wants to see what they look like. The two friends decide to sneak up a tunnel during the day to take a peep at a Hoo-Min. George, fascinated by the gigantic creature, follows it and has to be rescued by Belinda when the Hoo-Min tries to kill him. Despite a spanking from Belinda, George remains incorrigible.

When choking smoke fills the tunnels, the young centipedes climb the Up-Pipe knowing it is their only chance of escape. But Belinda is unable to follow. George and Harry find themselves in a Hoo-Min's bedroom and climb the bed leg to explore tunnels in the blankets and a big, warm meat mountain – a human foot! The two friends need to get damp to survive so climb along the human's body into its mouth. Two seconds later they are spat out and find themselves running around in bright light, being chased by a Hoo-Min with a rolled up newspaper. Luckily they find the shower and drop down the drain to land on the earth pile where Belinda is lying, looking like a very dead centipede.

The two friends push and pull Belinda back to the nest, where she sleeps her way to recovery while the friends go to the No-top-world to find food. They manage to avoid telling Belinda details of their encounter with the Hoo-Min but Belinda reveals that, when she and Harry's father went up the Up-Pipe, he was attacked by a Hoo-Min while allowing her to escape. He was never seen again. The two friends are left wishing they had managed to inflict at least one bite on the Hoo-Min in retaliation for the loss of Harry's father.

4

GUIDED READING – HARRY THE POISONOUS CENTIPEDE

APP Reading Links

Assessment Focus

AF1 - Session 1: Level 2/3
          Session 2: Level 3
AF3 - Session 1: Level 2
          Session 2: Level 2/3
AF5 - Session 1: Level 2
          Session 2: Level 3
AF6 - Session 1: Level 2
          Session 2: Level 3

Session 1 (AF1, AF3, AF5, AF6)

Book introduction

Ask children what they know about centipedes. List some of the ideas on a whiteboard for checking after reading. Why might the story make you squirm? Look at the picture of Harry's world on page 6. What else do you know about centipedes by looking at the diagram? Ask the children to note the vocabulary HOO-MIN and NO-TOP-WORLD. What is this suggesting? Why has the author written like this?

Strategy check

Remind children about the differences between reading aloud and reading silently. What strategies do they use when reading aloud? Will these be the same when they are reading silently? Explain to the children that some of the words have been made up but the meanings are clear. Ask them to note the invented words as they read.

Independent reading

Set the focus for reading – to identify those aspects of the story that make it seem familiar and almost human, contrasting with the techniques the author uses to suggest an alien world. Tell the children to read silently to themselves while each child reads a short section aloud in turn to the teacher. Ensure all strategies are being used to decode and make meaning from the text.

4

Return to the text

Ask children to locate the evidence that shows the centipedes have been invested with human characteristics. Include speech (p.8), typical relationship / conversation between mother and son (pp.11, 14-15, 19, 20-21), concern for the child's welfare (pp.35, 38). Ask the children to give some examples of invented words. Can they suggest what the words represent? Why do they think the author has written some words like this? Does it remind the children of language they have encountered anywhere else? Refer children to CM1 to record the vocabulary as they read on.

Response to text

Refer children to the bottom of pages 8 and 9. Read some of page 9 aloud, emphasising the author's clear involvement and knowledge. Note the use of the first person – *Which is why* I *call him Harry* – ...I *don't know. Why bother?* What effect does this style of writing have on the reader? Encourage children to express their own views. Does it make them more involved? Do they find the author's style of writing intrusive or amusing? Ask for reasons.

Next steps

Children can continue to use CM1 to list the invented words and their meanings. Use the information in the book to fill in a fact sheet about centipedes – CM2. Children read on independently in the text to the end of Chapter 19 (p.96) before the next guided reading session.

Session 2 (AF1, AF3, AF5, AF6)

Introduction

Ask the children to work in pairs to share their favourite part of the story so far. Which of Harry's adventures did they like best and why? Listen to some responses and direct children to the relevant sections of the text to make use of the illustrations to support their oral work.

Find passages where the author is commenting on the action and ask the children how this affects the way they read the story and how they respond to the characters.

Explore the relationship between Harry and George. Who is the leader? How do we know? How would the children have reacted if they had been Harry on page 82 or George on page 95? What do they think Belinda was feeling at this point in the story?

Strategy check

Check the lists of made up words. Do these add to the children's enjoyment of the story? Why? Explain the meaning of *incorrigible* (p.96). What other evidence is there that George is incorrigible? How does the author accentuate the threat to the centipedes on pages 84-86? Note use of italics, onomatopoeic words in capitals (WHACK!), use of punctuation, repeated words and illustrations. Think about how this would be read aloud. Does this have the same impact when read silently? Why?

Independent reading

Ask the children to notice how the illustrations support the text in the next chapters. Ask them to note how the centipedes behave when the smoke threatens to engulf them. Listen to each child read aloud and check that all strategies are being used.

Return to the text

Praise the use of strategies, expressive reading and pupils who take account of the punctuation to emphasise the mounting tension. Talk about the illustrations on pages 101-103. How do they suggest the centipedes are under threat?

Response to text

Notice how the author has slowed down the pace of the narrative on page 104. How and why has she done this? Look at the use of the punctuation, repetition, italics and experiment with the tone in which some of these sentences would be read. Encourage children to pick out the adverbs – *slowly, at last, hanging his little round head, sadly*. Demonstrate how the words would be spoken by role-playing parts of the conversation.

Ask children to predict the ending. Why do they think Belinda doesn't want them to go up the Up-Pipe. What will happen to her? Note the invented words as the centipedes enter the Hoo-Min's bedroom. Ask the children to say what they would tell their friends about this book.

Next steps

Finish reading the book and write a short review for other pupils in the class on CM3, using some of the ideas from the last reading session. Use CM4 for the children to record their feelings at various points in the story. Ask them to explain how and why the author influenced their feelings. In pairs, act out one of George and Harry's adventures. Some groups of three could do the same and add in Belinda's role.

4

Writing opportunities

- Write a message to your friend in Centipedish.
- Write one of the adventures as a short play script.
- Write a set of instructions for humans – what to do if you see a centipede.
- Create a fact-file for another minibeast, using reference books or the internet to find information.
- Draw a picture of a centipede and label its various parts.
- Write a blurb for the back of the book.
- Create a comic strip style picture story of one of the adventures, using speech bubbles and a little text.

Harry the Poisonous Centipede (1)

Name . . . . Date . . . .

Centipedish or English?

Page	Word made up or used by the author	Meaning in our language
5	Hoo-Min	human
5	No-top-world	above ground

Name . . . . Date. . . . .

Fact-file - Centipedes

Fill in information about centipedes by referring to the book. Add illustrations to support your notes.

Facts	Belinda	Harry	Page
Appearance			
Food			
Habitat			
Predators			
Communication			

Name . . . . Date . . . .

Book review

Characters

Settings

Main events

How it makes you feel

Reasons why your friends should read the book

Name. . . . . Date. . . . .

Feelings chart

How did you feel when you read these pages?
How did the author influence your feelings?

Page	Feelings	Reasons for your feelings
Pages 20-23 'The Warning'		
Pages 27-29 Harry almost drowns		
Pages 45-50 George to the rescue		
Pages 127-132 'The Lovely Wet Tunnel'		
Pages 144-146 'The Long Way Home'		
Pages 156-160 'A New World'		

The Pea and the Princess *by Mini Grey*
Level 2A>3

SUMMARY OF THE STORY

This is a modern retelling of a traditional fairytale. The story is told from the pea's point of view and traces its life from the Palace garden through to the Palace kitchen where it is selected by the Queen to help her to find a real Princess to marry her son.

Scenes from the royal garden and allotment appear as endpapers; they form an important part of the story by introducing the main characters in the story – two contrasting families. The Queen and her son, the Prince, are placed on one side of the wall, while the working girl and her parents are on the other.

The Queen wants her thirty-four-year-old son to find a wife but, even after a year of travelling the Known World, the Prince is unable to find a suitable Princess to marry. The Queen places the pea under twenty mattresses and feather beds, telling the Prince that he is going to marry the first girl who can feel it.

Various princesses spend the night on top of the mattresses but all are too polite to say they have had an uncomfortable night. When the girl from the garden arrives at the palace one wet and stormy night and is put to bed, the pea decides to take matters into its own hands. It spends the night whispering in the girl's ear, telling her she is very uncomfortable.

The next morning, the girl tells the Queen that she has spent an awful night. The Prince is delighted to have found a wife. The wedding is arranged, the two families are united, the pea becomes a very important artefact and the Palace allotment flourishes as the newly-weds work in it together.

GUIDED READING – THE PEA AND THE PRINCESS

APP Reading Links

Assessment Focus

AF1 - Session 1: Level 3
        Session 2: Level 2/3
AF3 - Session 1: Level 2/3
        Session 2: Level 2/3
AF5 - Session 2: Level 2/3
AF6 - Session 1: Level 2/3
        Session 2: Level 2/3
AF7 - Session 1: Level 2/3
        Session 2: Level 3

Session 1 (AF1, AF3, AF6, AF7)

Book introduction

Discuss the cover of the book. Ask the children what sort of story they think it is. Ask for reasons for their choice. Do they know another story like this? They may have read *The Princess and the Pea*. Ask what happened in that story. Make predictions about the events of this story. Look at the back cover of the book. What evidence is there that this story has been told before?

Strategy check

Ask children to look at the frontispiece and describe what they see. Introduce the word contrast and check meaning. Guide them to notice the contrast between the garden (productive and open) and the maze (formal and enclosed). Note separating wall with gate firmly closed. Why? Identify contrasts in characters on each side of the double page. Remind children of the importance of using the pictures as a cueing strategy to support their understanding of the text and check that other cueing strategies (searchlights) are known. Demonstrate the use of the searchlights using the first two pages of the text. Check children's understanding of the word *allotment*.

Independent reading

Ask children to read independently, thinking about the following as they do so: Who is telling the story? How do we know? The pea is going to be important. How do we know? In what way is it important? While the children read, listen to each child, checking the cueing strategies. Praise their attempts to work out unfamiliar words.

Return to the text

Praise children's use of the pictures to help them to work out unfamiliar words and refer to pages where the pictures were particularly useful – e.g. page 4 where the pea is in the box, surrounded by soft tissue to protect it. Talk about the questions posed before the independent reading session. Ask children to justify their answers by reference to the text.

Response to text

Would you expect a pea to be a storyteller? Are you surprised the pea is telling the story? Why? How does it affect the story? Guide children to the idea that the pea is involved in the events as they happen; it has first-hand experience and the story is autobiographical. It makes the story more convincing. Recap on the contrasts from the beginning of the book and identify the different characteristics of the various princesses.

Focus on the Queen and her son by reading the speech on pages 6 and 8. Adopt a bossy, authoritative voice for the Queen and a milder, subservient tone for her son as he agrees to search for a wife. Ask the children to demonstrate how they would say these words. It will be more effective if children adopt the stance of the Queen (p.5) – standing, arms folded, scowling expression – to allow them to 'feel' the character.

Next steps

Ask the children to finish reading the text before the next session. They could read independently or in pairs, supporting one another to use the searchlights. Explain how to use CM1 or CM2, using the text to support them.

Session 2 (AF1, AF3, AF5, AF6, AF7)

Introduction

Refer to pages 11 and 12. Identify what is happening in this part of the story. Ask the children to role-play the scene between the Queen and her son. Adopt the poses; the 'Queen' speaks the words from the text. What is the Prince feeling at this point? Fed up, glum, frustrated. What would you be feeling? How has the author suggested these feelings? Ask the same questions of the Queen. She is exasperated, annoyed and desperate. This should be evident from the expression as the children read aloud.

Revisit the contrast between the characters. Include the girl outside the window; she is working and smiling, the Prince is bored and unhappy. Ask the children to use their completed CM2 sheets and share some of the contrasts they have found in the text. Why has the author introduced these contrasts? What is she trying to convey?

Strategy check

Identify how the author has suggested characteristics through speech and the use of verbs telling the reader how the words are spoken. Use page 15 to demonstrate how the polite princesses speak; identify verbs – gasped (p.18); whispered (p.19); sighed (p.22). Teach children strategies for reading these words, if necessary. Then ask children to speak in these ways.

Independent reading

All children practise reading sections of text where there is speech. Use expression and intonation to ensure the feelings of the characters are conveyed to the listener. Children could be given different sections of the text or they could choose which character they want to be. Listen to each child as they practise, check reading strategies are being used and ensure expressive reading.

After a few minutes, ask children to share their reading with a partner in the group.

Return to the text

Hear some of the conversations/speeches read aloud. Ask the children how the words and the expression work together to create an impression of the character. Refer to page 24, where the pea is speaking. Hear some children read these words aloud. Ensure they bring out the self-importance of the pea.

What else does the author use to support the way these words should be read? Use of short sentences, capitals, text working with the picture, directly addresses the reader – *if you visit… you may chance to see me.*

Response to text

What are the themes in this book? Link to contrasts – rich / poor, aristocracy / workers, different homes and lifestyles – so children recognise separateness leading to final unity; similarities with current royal family; almost magical intervention of fate – the storm washing away the old order of things to make way for the new can be linked with how circumstances and events affect our lives. Make this relevant to the children by referring to something that has happened in school or at home and asking them to describe it. For instance, a new child may have joined the school because his parents had to move to the area – a parent may have got a new job. In extreme circumstances, something may have affected the school building – lightning, fire, damp or building work and the children have had to move into temporary classrooms, then a wonderful new building.

Conclude by asking children in pairs to compare the frontispiece with the end paper. Each pair to identify two differences and say what the author is trying to imply or tell us about the characters and their lives through these contrasts. Some ideas could be: colours, the season is different, plants are thriving, the doors are open – suggesting the unification of the two worlds, prince and princess working together – no class difference, Queen is enclosed in the maze – why? Ask each child in turn to say what they have enjoyed about the story and why.

Next steps

Leave the book available to be re-read or taken home. If possible, provide other books by the same author in the reading area and supply a copy of The Princess and the Pea for children to read independently for comparison. Use CM3 and CM4 for independent or group work.

5

Writing opportunities

- Re-write the story from the girl's point of view.
- What happened next? Write a sequel to the story, using the end piece as a starting point. (Note the expression of the Queen, the open door in the wall and the contrast between the first picture and this one.)
- Create a set of instructions – How to Grow Vegetables or How to Look After your Garden/Allotment.
- Trace the fictitious journey of the Prince as he looks for a Princess. Draw a map of the Known World and place each of the princesses into a context on it.
- Write a leaflet giving information about the pea for visitors to the museum.
- Re-write the scene between the Queen and the Prince as a play script; ensure the characteristics of each are suggested through the words spoken, the expression and the stage directions.
- Write a short review of this book for other children in your class. Include your opinion, with reasons, and give the book a rating out of ten.

5 The Pea and the Princess (1)

Name . . . . Date. . . . .

PRINCESSES

The Prince met many princesses. Think of some words and phrases to describe them. Add some princesses of your own.

Too loud
bossy
noisy
shouts a lot
screams
orders people about

Too sleepy

Too scruffy

Too grumpy

Too

Too

Name . . . . Date. . . . .

CONTRASTS

Identify some of the contrasts in the book and record them using words or pictures.

Page	Contrasts	

5 The Pea and the Princess (3)

Name . . . . Date . . . .

COMPARING STORIES

Title and author	Main events	Characters	Illustrations	Themes

The book I like best is...

because...

Name . . . . Date . . . .

STORY GRAMMAR

Title:	Characters
Author:	
Publisher:	

Plot	Setting

Special Features	Themes

SUMMARY OF THE STORY

Winnie the Witch takes delivery of a new computer. She is very excited as she logs on to the internet to order a new wand but Wilbur, the cat, is confused by the mouse. When he tries to pat it, Winnie puts him outside in the rain. She doesn't notice him getting wetter and wetter as she plays on the computer. Wilbur is convinced that the mouse has put a spell on her.

When rain begins to drip through the roof and threatens to spoil the new computer, Winnie has problems finding her wand and her book of spells to stop the leak. She decides to scan all her spells into the computer so she can locate them with one click. Having tested the procedure on Wilbur by turning him blue, Winnie throws away her book and wand in the dustbin.

That evening, Wilbur decides to investigate the mouse. During the night, he manages to make both himself and the computer disappear. When she discovers this the next morning, Winnie searches in vain for her spell book and wand. She remembers where she put them just as the dustcart is driving away.

In the nick of time, the new wand arrives and Winnie is able to recover her book of spells and look up the spell to make things reappear. The computer and Wilbur are restored and Winnie decides to keep her book of spells and her magic wand in case she needs them another day.

GUIDED READING – WINNIE'S NEW COMPUTER

APP Reading Links

Assessment Focus

AF1 - Session 1: 1/2
           Session 2: Level 3
AF3 - Session 1: Level 2/3
           Session 2: Level 3
AF5 - Session 1: Level 2
           Session 2: Level 3
AF6 - Session 1: Level 2/3
           Session 2: Level 2/3
AF7 - Session 1: Level 2/3
           Session 2: Level 3

Session 1 (AF1, AF3, AF5, AF6, AF7)

Book introduction

Share the cover. Discuss in relation to other 'witch' books the children may have read. Identify the two main characters. Ask the children to look at their body positions and expressions and say what they think the characters are feeling. Draw out the contrast – Winnie is happy and excited, Wilbur is horrified and tense. Ask for reasons why they should feel like this. How would they feel if they had just received a new computer?

Strategy check

Ask the children to suggest vocabulary related to computers that might be in the book. Guide them to words such as *click, mouse, internet, websites, scan, load.* Ask them how websites would be written down. Use www.oup.com/winnie as an example as this can be used later for follow-up activities and reading. Check children understand the meaning of the technical vocabulary. They could be asked to demonstrate the words or put them into sentences.

Demonstrate how to break up words into smaller chunks to read them: *in-ter-net* or *web-site.* Ask children to use this strategy with *abracadabra, remembered.*

Independent reading

Tell the children they are going to look at the pictures on each page and talk to a partner about what is happening in each one, focusing specifically on the characters.

The focus for this session is to identify how the illustrator has created humour through the pictures as well as articulating what is happening in the plot of the story. Ask the children to find Wilbur in each of the pictures and say what he is doing and feeling at various points in the story. They could record their ideas on large Post-it notes.

While the children talk to one another, the teacher will listen and support, pointing out humorous features and helping them to find Wilbur and generate words and phrases to describe him.

Return to the text

Ask children in turn to describe briefly what is happening on each page. The purpose is to get an outline of the story and to locate Wilbur and describe his feelings and features.

His reaction to the main events can be seen clearly, particularly when he stares at the mouse and licks his lips, when he is outside in the rain and when he is allowed back in, turned blue then back to black.

Response to text

Ask the children how the illustrator has created humour. Note the different sizes of picture, the settings, the expressions on the characters' faces, the inclusion of details such as other creatures, Winnie's clothes, the style of the house, colours, different fonts and words such as *plop, zap, wandsRus*.

Introduce CM1 and demonstrate how to complete the sections.

Next steps

Read the book, individually or in pairs, and fill in CM1, outlining the plot.

Session 2 (AF1, AF3, AF5, AF6, AF7)

Introduction

Ask children to talk through their completed CM1 sheets. Link events, problems and resolutions and identify how suspense is built up in the story.

Strategy check

Ask if the children encountered any difficulties reading the text. Support the reading by reminding children of the strategies (searchlights) to use for unfamiliar words. Re-read any sections of text they found difficult.

Look at the text on page 3 and ask a child to read the words aloud. Concentrate on the line 'Is that a *mouse*? thought Wilbur.' Why is the word mouse in italics? How should the line be read?

Look at the words spoken by Winnie on the next page. Practise reading them, taking account of the punctuation.

On page 7, italics have been used again. What is the reason for this? How does it affect the way the lines are read. How does this add to the humour?

What do the children notice about the sentences? They are mostly short and simple – one clause. Why do they think the author has written like this? Draw out that longer sentences are unnecessary when so much information is given through the pictures.

6

Independent reading

Before starting the independent work, demonstrate how to use one of the interview cards from CM2 and CM3. The children then work in pairs. One child from each pair selects an interview card and reads it to their partner, who responds, making reference to the text. The second child from the pair repeats the process with another card. This continues until most cards have been used.

Return to the text

Each pair chooses one card each to demonstrate the question and answer to the rest of the group.

Response to text

Use some of the answers to the questions to develop children's responses further. Ask for further clarification or specific text references using question starts such as: *Why do you think..., Which words or phrases..., How does the writer..., What made this story..., What or how did you feel when...?*

Next steps

Visit Winnie at www.oup.com/winnie. You will find a quiz based on Winnie's New Computer, together with the jokes that Winnie found when she was playing on her computer, profiles of the author and illustrator, reviews and activities relating to the other titles in the series.

Read and compare some other books about witches. Use CM4 to record comparisons. Some titles could be:

Room on the Broom by Julia Donaldson
The Worst Witch series by Jill Murphy
The Witches by Roald Dahl
The Meg and Mog series by Helen Nicoll and Jan Pienkowski – all Picture Puffins.

Writing opportunities

- Re-tell the story from Wilbur's point of view.
- Write the rules for using and looking after a new computer for Winnie.
- Write a book of spells for Winnie.
- Create Wilbur's diary. Add in some of his thoughts and feelings about Winnie and her various exploits.
- Write another adventure for Winnie and Wilbur.
- Write a set of instructions for Winnie, telling her how to look after Wilbur.

6 Winnie's New Computer (1)

Name . . . . Date . . . .

Identify the main events in the book.

Setting	Inside and outside Winnie's black house. It has turrets, chimneys and lots of windows. Inside it is very untidy.
Characters	
Opening event	Winnie's new computer arrives and she uses it to order a new wand. Wilbur is very suspicious of the mouse.
Problem 1	
Resolution	
Events	Winnie puts all her spells on the computer and throws away her wand and book of spells.
Problem 2	
Resolution	
Conclusion	Winnie uses the computer to cast spells but decides to keep her book of spells and her wand in case she needs them another day.

Interview cards (1)

When you looked at the cover of this book, what made you want to read it?	Would you like to live in a house like Winnie's? Give two reasons for your answer.
Which character had the problems? How did she solve them?	How do the authors of this book try to make you laugh? Choose one page where they succeed and talk about it.
Show me the page you liked best. Read it to me. Tell me why you liked it?	What would you say to a friend who wanted to read this book?

Interview cards (2)

Is there anything you would change if you were writing this book? Give your reasons.	If you were Wilbur and you could talk, what would you say to Winnie at the end of the story?
Which were the most exciting parts of the story? Read me the pages. Why were they exciting?	Has anything like this ever happened to you? Tell me about it.
Tell me three facts about Winnie without looking at the book again.	Do you think Winnie was right to scan her spells into the computer? Why is it important to have books as well?

Name . . . . Date . . . .

Comparison of stories about witches

Read some other books that have a witch as a main character and compare them.

Title and author of book	Picture of witch	Main events	Rating /10

The Enormous Crocodile *by Roald Dahl*
Level 2A>3

SUMMARY OF THE STORY

A greedy crocodile is boasting to his friend, the Notsobig Crocodile, that he can devise various secret plans and clever tricks to catch some juicy small children to satisfy his voracious appetite. He leaves the brown, muddy river and meets various animals as he walks through the jungle – Humpy-Rumpy the hippopotamus, Trunky the elephant, Muggle-Wump the monkey and the Roly-Poly Bird. The animals all know that the Enormous Crocodile has nasty plans and nasty tricks in mind; they are horrified that he is going to eat small children but they are all cleverer than he is.

As he enters the town, the Enormous Crocodile pretends to be a coconut tree. Just as a small boy is about to climb the 'tree', Humpty-Rumpty charges in and knocks the Enormous Crocodile to the ground.

However, crocodiles are tough. Clever Trick Number Two is to make himself into a see-saw by balancing himself over a piece of wood in the playground. Just as the children are about to sit on the 'see-saw', Muggle-Wump appears and tells the children to run away as the crocodile is about to eat them up.

Thwarted again, the Enormous Crocodile approaches a roundabout at the fair to pose as a wooden crocodile. A girl is about to climb up to ride on him when the Roly-Poly Bird swooshes down and tells her it is a real crocodile who wants to eat her up.

By now the Enormous Crocodile is very hungry. Clever Trick Number Four is to place himself as a picnic bench next to a table on which he has placed flowers to entice the children. He waits as the children approach. They are about to sit on his back when a loud voice bellows 'Stand back!' Trunky the Elephant crashes out of the bushes, trots over to the crocodile bench and wraps his trunk around the crocodile's tail.

As he dangles upside down, Trunky swings the crocodile round and round in the air, faster and faster. He suddenly lets go and the crocodile sails up into the sky 'like a huge green rocket'. Higher and faster he goes, past the moon and stars, until he crashes headlong into the sun and sizzles up 'like a sausage'.

7

Guided Reading – The Enormous Crocodile

APP Reading Links

Assessment Focus

AF1 - Session 1: Level 2/3
         Session 2: Level 2/3
AF3 - Session 1: Level 2/3
         Session 2: Level 3
AF4 - Session 1: Level 2
         Session 2: Level 2
AF5 - Session 1: Level 2/3
         Session 2: Level 2/3
AF6 - Session 1: Level 2
         Session 2: Level 3

Session 1 (AF1, AF3, AF4, AF5, AF6)

Book introduction

Ask the children about the author and illustrator. Have they seen or read any other books by either of these two. Show the children some titles such as The Magic Finger by Roald Dahl and ask for a brief synopsis of that story to use as a comparison with this one. What type of stories does Roald Dahl write?

Read the blurb together. Ask the children to describe a 'clever trick' they think the crocodile might use to catch some children to eat. Ask the children where crocodiles live. Identify some other jungle animals that might be in the story. Do they think crocodiles are clever? Give reasons.

Strategy check

Read pages 9 and 10 aloud to the children, emphasising the way the two crocodiles are talking. Take account of the punctuation, the verbs and the italics. Emphasise the words to suggest the different views of the two crocodiles. Ask the children why you emphasised *tough* and *chewy, nasty* and *bitter*. Select some children to read the words spoken by the two crocodiles on page 10 as if they are having the conversation. Remind the children to read with expression, taking account of the punctuation when they are reading to themselves.

Independent reading

Ask the children to begin reading silently at page 11 and to look out for punctuation marks, italics and verbs to indicate the way the words are spoken. Remind children of the strategies to use when they are reading. Listen to each child read aloud. Prompt them to read the spoken words with expression.

Return to the text

Praise the children's reading. Direct them to page 12 and ask a child to read the Notsobig One's words aloud. How would he say these words? What does it suggest about his feelings for the Enormous Crocodile? Do the same with the conversation between the Enormous Crocodile and Humpty-Rumpy at the top of page 16. Emphasise really and discuss the author's use of the ellipsis in 'You don't mean…' Ask two children to read the conversation up to 'crocodile soup'.

Point out that how a character speaks helps the reader to build up a fuller picture of him. E.g. page 24 "'Nasty!' cried the Crocodile. 'Of course it's not nasty! It's delicious!'" How would these words be spoken and what does it suggest about the crocodile?

Response to text

Refer children to the description of the crocodile at the top of page 12. Notice the descriptive vocabulary and the simile. Why do the children think the author has compared the teeth to knives?

Ask the children to scan some of the pages they have read and find some more examples of descriptive language – real and invented. Some could be *biggest, brownest muddiest river* (p.9); *fat juicy little child* (p.10); the rhymes on pages 15, 17, 20 and 26; *horrid greedy grumptious brute* (p.16); *foul and filthy fiend* (p.18) and *squashed and squished and squizzled* (p.18). If appropriate, introduce the term alliteration and encourage children to find more examples of it as they read on independently.

Why has the author listed adjectives to describe nouns? How does he intend the reader to feel? Does it work? How do the children feel?

Ask each child in turn what they think is going to happen in the rest of the story and why. Are there any clues in the text that make them think of a particular ending? Is the story similar to another one they have read where the main character boasts about his cleverness?

7

Ask the children what they think will happen in the end. Will the Enormous Crocodile eat any children? What will the other animals do? Are there any clues in the text or pictures that might help them to predict the ending of the story? Record children's predictions on a whiteboard or flip chart ready for the next session. Ensure they offer reasons for their prediction.

Next steps
Children read on in the book, keeping a record of descriptive language and similes on CM1. Encourage them to say why the author has used these words and phrases. Suggest children work in pairs to complete their lists. Children begin to use CM2 to map the main events in the stories.

Session 2 (AF1, AF3, AF4, AF5, AF6)

Introduction
Ask the children to share some examples of descriptive language. Expect them to refer to the page, read the example aloud and say what the effect is. Encourage discussion among the children. Some may have different opinions about what works. Remind children of similes and alliteration. Value all contributions.

Strategy check
Remind the children about how they read some of the speech and the verbs that were used instead of said. Help the children to locate some verbs and explain meanings. Identify descriptive verbs on the lists they have made on CM1. Look at some examples that are used: *snapped* (p.26); *peered* (p.31); *crashing and snorting* (p.33); *waddled* (p.37); *swishing and swooshing* (p.40); *bellowed* (p.51); *yelled* (p.51). Explain meanings if necessary.

Independent reading
Ask children to read to the end of the book. If they have already finished it before this second session, ask them to read aloud to one another, taking a character each and reading with expression. The focus for reading is to think about reading aloud for an audience. Practise reading page 52 to the end to make the story sound exciting and dramatic.

Return to the text

Listen to children read the end section of the book. How has the author made them read in a certain way? Note use of capitals, minimal text on a page alongside larger dramatic pictures, spacing of text, use of descriptive language such as *blurry circle* (p.55); *shooting high up into the sky like a huge green rocket* (p.56); repetition (p.58); *crashed, sizzled up like a sausage* and view of space on the last page. How accurate were the children's predictions for the end of the story? Did they expect the crocodile to be punished? Did they expect some children to be eaten? Ask the children to justify their answers from the text or from what they know of other stories by this author.

Response to text

Compare children's predictions about the ending from the previous session with the actual ending. Do they like the ending? Give reasons. How do they feel about the crocodile now? Would their feelings be different if they were the children in the story who had almost been eaten by it?

What do they think the Notsobig Crocodile would have said to the other jungle animals at the end of the story? Ask the children in turn to give an opinion about the story. Suggest some starters such as *I liked the story because...* or *The book made me feel...* or *This is like another story I know called...* or *I think the crocodile deserved to be fried because...*

Next steps

Complete the grid showing the story's main events using CM2, then encourage the children to make personal responses to the text by answering the questions on CM3. Use CM4 for children to formulate some questions they would like to ask the author then visit www.roalddahl.com to read about the author to find some answers, explore some of his other texts and attempt some quizzes. Using information already gained and recorded on the previous CMs, children can prepare a talk for the class about Roald Dahl.

Writing opportunities
- Use some of the rhymes in the text as models for writing own rhymes.
- Create a book of disguises for crocodiles.
- Write an alternative ending to the story.
- Write part of the story from the point of view of one of the other animals.
- Write a list of rules for good behaviour for the crocodile.
- Write part of the story as a play script.

7 The Enormous Crocodile (1)

Name . . . . Date. . . . .

EXAMPLES OF DESCRIPTIVE LANGUAGE

Page	Examples of descriptive words and phrases	Say what the words are describing and why you think the author has used them

Name . . . . Date. . . . .

MAIN EVENTS

Draw a picture of each nasty trick, say what the children do and describe how they are saved.

Nasty tricks	What the children do?	Which animal saves the children and what does it do?
One		
Two		
Three		
Four		

7 The Enormous Crocodile (3)

Name . . . . Date. . . . .

QUIZ

1) Which of the jungle animals do you think is the cleverest and why?

2) What do you think Mary and Toto would have said to their friends when they got back to the town?

3) Which was the most effective disguise that the crocodile used and why?

4) How did you feel about the crocodile at the end of the story and why?

7 The Magic Finger (4)

Name . . . . Date. . . . .

Work with a partner to write some questions that you would like to ask the author. Write them here.

Question 1:

Question 2:

Question 3:

Now visit www.roalddahl.com – the author's website – to find the answers to some of your questions.

Dinosaur School *by Dick-King Smith*
Level 3

SUMMARY OF THE STORY

Basil Brontosaurus is teased at playschool by all the other little dinosaurs, who call him stupid. His mother tells him he's special because he has two brains - one in his head and one in the middle of his back. This cheers Basil up but unfortunately he now not only thinks he is twice as clever as the others he thinks he's twice as big as them. Basil takes his revenge by becoming a bully. His parents try to tell him to be careful otherwise he will get himself into trouble. Basil doesn't listen to his parents and is expelled from playschool. Basil doesn't care. He is very boastful and thinks he is better than all the other dinosaurs. Then he meets a small Tyrannosaurus rex who tells him that Tyrannosaurus rex eat brontosauruses. Basil is unimpressed but then along comes the little T- rex's father. Basil lumbers away in terror. His mother and father say they hope he has learnt his lesson and that if he wants to grow up to be as big as his father he must always remember to use his brains.

GUIDED READING – DINOSAUR SCHOOL

APP Reading Links

Assessment Focus

AF1 - Session 1: Level 2/3
      Session 2: Level 3
AF2 - Session 1: Level 3
      Session 2: Level 3
AF3 - Session 1: Level 2/3
      Session 2: Level 3
AF6 - Session 1: Level 2/3
      Session 2: Level 3
AF7 - Session 1: Level 3
      Session 2: Level 3

Session 1 (AF1, AF2, AF3, AF6, AF7)

Book introduction
Ask the children to look at the front cover to identify the author of the book. Check if any of them have read 'The Sheep-Pig' or seen the film it inspired – Babe. Tell the children that Dick King-Smith was famous for writing stories about animals. Ask them what kind of animals are going to feature in this story. Now have the children read the blurb on the back. Discuss what they think the secret that makes Basil "very special at school" could be.

Strategy check

Point out that any book featuring dinosaurs is going to have some long and potentially difficult words in it. Read the first two pages of Dinosaur School aloud to the children. Highlight the multi-syllabic words being used. Model some effective strategies for decoding these words and any others that they may encounter in the text. For example they can:

- sound the word out by starting with the first letter and then saying each letter-sound out loud.
- blend the sounds together and try to say the word. Then they can see if the word makes sense in the sentence.
- look for familiar letter chunks such as sound/symbols, prefixes, suffixes, endings, whole words, or base words. Then they can read each chunk by itself and blend the chunks together and sound out the word. Now they can see if that word make sense in the sentence.

Independent reading

Ask the children to read up to the part of the story where Herb tells Araminta that he mostly talked about waterweed with his gang down in the swamp. Remind them to use the decoding strategies you have discussed if they meet any difficult or unfamiliar words. Listen to individual readers and praise them for their efforts in applying appropriate reading strategies.

Return to the text

Ask the children how the author shows that Basil's father, Herb is not a very quick thinker? Why does Basil's mother take him to a quiet spot? What is the secret that every brontosaurus is told by their parents when they are old enough? Why does Basil's mother think that knowing the secret will stop Basil being a "cry-baby"?

Ask the children how Basil behaves at school after his mother tells him the secret? Encourage them to support their answers with evidence from the text. What do they think Basil means when he says "actions speak louder than words"? Why does Basil's teacher come to see his mother and father? How do we know that Herb isn't very sympathetic about Basil crying at school? What evidence is there in the text that Herb has a very short memory? Who does Basil's mother blame for Basil becoming a bully? Why?

8

Response to text

Ask the children if they feel sorry for Basil when they first read about him? Why? Why not? Why do they think Basil's mother tells him about his extra brain? Ask the children if they are surprised that Basil behaves like a bully? Have them give reasons for their response. What do the children feel about Herb, Araminta and Basil? What kind of characters are they? Are they good parents? Are they clever, silly, or just not very interested in anything except eating waterweed? Why do the children think the author has written about these characters in the way he has? Do the children like them? Why? Why not?

Next steps

Talk with the children about their memories of their first day at school. Was it a happy time for them? Why? Why not? Using clues from the text, encourage them to imagine what Basil's first day at playschool was like. Now ask them to write a diary entry for Basil describing his feelings about his first day at the playschool.

Have the children complete CM1, a character profile of Herb and Araminta.

Session 2 (AF1, AF2, AF3, AF6, AF7)

Introduction

Talk to the children about the usual fate of bullies in stories. Ask them what they think will happen to Basil? Do they think he will see the error of his ways? Do they think the story will have a happy ending? Have them give you reasons for their predictions.

Strategy check

Explain that skim reading is a very useful reading strategy as it allows you to find specific information quickly. Show the children how to skim read by modelling reading from page 16 to half way down page 19 quickly looking for evidence showing that Basil has become a very unsympathetic character. List the evidence and discuss how this is the author's way of alerting the reader that the conceited young dinosaur is heading for a fall.

Independent reading

Ask the children to read to the end of the story. Ask them to note how the author uses humour when describing Basil's meeting with the Tyrannosaurus.

Return to the text

Why is Basil rude to the smallish dinosaur he meets? What clues are there in the author's description of the new dinosaur that tell us that Basil should be very wary of it? Why doesn't Basil think much of this new dinosaur? How do Basil's two brains help him to escape from the big Tyrannosaurus? Why doesn't the Tyrannosaurus catch Basil? What unusual word does Araminta use to describe Basil's agitated state? What advice does Araminta give to Basil to keep him safe in future? What evidence is there in the text that shows Herb thinks his own joke is funny?

Response to text

Do you think Basil is right to feel so pleased with himself? Why? Why not? What do you think the Tyrannosaurus thinks of Basil? Why do you think this? How would you feel if you suddenly came face to face with a big Tyrannosaurus? Do you think Basil has learnt his lesson? Did you find Herb's joke funny? Why? Why not? What do you think of the ending of the story? Why?

Next steps

Talk with the children about why the teacher expelled Basil from playschool. Do they think she is being fair to Basil? Have them refer back to the text to look for reasons to explain her actions. Now have them write the letter in CM3.

Remind them that Basil actually has two brains and they'll need to remember this when completing CM4.

Writing opportunities
- Write a fact file for a Tyrannosaurus rex.
- Write a project book about dinosaurs.
- Write ten questions for a dinosaur quiz.

Name . . . . Date. . . . .

My First day at Playschool

Imagine you are Basil. Write an entry in your diary saying what happened on your first day at playschool. Were you happy? Did you like the other young dinosaurs? Was your teacher kind? What did you learn?

Dear Diary

Name . . . . Date. . . . .

Character Profile

Write a character profile card for Herb and Araminta.

Physical description (Herb):

Likes:

Dislikes:

Speed:

Brain power (marks out of 10):

Physical description (Araminta):

Likes:

Dislikes:

Speed:

Brain power (marks out of 10):

Name . . . . Date. . . . .

School's Out

Write a letter from the playschool teacher to Basil's mother and father explaining why she is going to expel him from playschool.

Diddy Dinos Playschool

Dear Mr and Mrs Brontosaurus,

I am sorry to have to tell you that

Name . . . . Date. . . . .

Pride Comes Before a Fall

Draw a picture showing what happened when Basil met the big Tyrannosaurus rex. Have thought bubbles coming out of each of the dinosaur's heads. Does the big T-rex think that Basil looks like a tasty snack? What are Basil's two brains telling him to do? Is the little T-rex thinking his Dad will teach the stuck-up brontosaurus a lesson?

Pup on the Pitch *by Sophie Smiley*
Level 3

SUMMARY OF THE STORY

Chapter 1
Bobby and his family are football mad. Bobby wants a pet. His Mum and Dad buy him a fish. He calls it Goal Fish but Bobby still wants a dog. Mr Maskell, Bobby's elderly neighbour gets a dog to help him with his chores. He agrees to share the pup with Bobby. Bobby thinks Davy Dog will be his special friend.

Chapter 2
Davy Dog is very naughty. He eats all Mum's cake. He chews up Bobby and his sister Charlie's things. They try to teach him to play football. Davy bursts the ball and messes on Bobby's goalie top. Bobby shows Davy the red card. Davy nips Bobby on the nose and piddles on his lap. Bobby thinks all dogs are monsters.

Chapter 3
Bobby who is usually very brave is now fearful. All dogs scare him. He has Down's syndrome. A poodle frightens him while he is waiting for his taxi to take him to his special school. He thinks if he covers his face no one will be able to see him. Kevin the bully arrives. He scares Bobby by barking at him.

Chapter 4
Charlie is hot tempered. Bullies like Kevin make her mad but she knows fighting him is wrong. When Dad, Charlie and Bobby are walking home from school, Bobby is scared by a fierce guard dog. Charlie kicks a can for the dog to chase. She makes a joke that the dog is a useless goalie but Bobby is still very scared.

Chapter 5
Bobby has changed. Anything to do with dogs terrifies him. The family all go to the big match. Bobby starts to cheer up. Then Kevin the bully causes trouble. Bobby is knocked over by two police dogs. He panics. Charlie can't get to him. Kevin sees his chance to make things worse. Luckily, Bobby's brother Wembley shoves Kevin aside and scoops Bobby up onto his shoulders. When they arrive home Bobby refuses to go out again.

Chapter 6
Bobby refuses to leave the house. He won't go to school. He won't even go into the garden in case Davy Dog is out there. Davy Dog is going to dog training lessons. Mum and Dad try everything they can but nothing will bring Bobby out of his shell. Charlie is sure the team she plays for will lose the big match if Bobby isn't there to cheer her on.

Chapter 7

On the day of Charlie's big match she persuades Bobby to come and watch her by telling him that if he covers his face with something dogs won't be able to see him. Bobby puts on a mask. He now thinks he is invisible. Charlie plays badly. She is worried about Bobby. Bobby is getting more and more frightened.

Chapter 8

Kevin turns up at the match riding his bike. He rides towards Bobby but then heads towards a new victim. Charlie is relieved. Then a dog barks and Bobby calls out for her to help. Kevin is heading towards Mr Maskell. Charlie doesn't know what to do. She stays on the pitch and scores a goal but she feels she has let her brother and Mr Maskell down.

Chapter 9

Charlie's team win the game. They are the Champions. Charlie sees Kevin bullying Mr Maskell. She goes to stop him but she trips over. Then she sees an amazing sight. Bobby and Davy Dog team up and flatten Kevin. Kevin is terrified. Bobby makes him apologise to Mr Maskell. Bobby and Davy Dog make friends. Davy has been trained and Bobby is no longer frightened of him. Bobby, Charlie and Davy run off to play football together.

GUIDED READING – PUP ON THE PITCH

APP Reading Links

Assessment Focus

AF2 - Session 1: Level 3
       Session 2: Level 3
AF3 - Session 1: Level 3
       Session 2: Level 3
AF6 - Session 1: Level 3
       Session 2: Level 3

Session 1 (AF2, AF3, AF6)

Book introduction

Before asking the children to read Pup on the Pitch look at the cover art with them and talk about what they think the subject of the story will be. Read the blurb on the back cover with them. What catches their interest and excites them about the book?

Strategy check

Point out that the blurb poses several questions about what might happen during the course of the story. For example, Can Bobby overcome his fear of dogs? Ask the children to look for the answers to these questions as they read the book. Encourage them to pause and write down the answers when they discover them.

Independent reading

Ask the children to read up to the end of Chapter 4. Tell them to focus on how and why Bobby changes from being a happy, football mad boy who wants a dog of his own into a withdrawn and frightened child who is terrified of dogs.

Return to the text

Chapter 1

Ask the children to tell you why Bobby wants a real live Davy Dog. Why doesn't Goal Fish meet Bobby's needs? Why does Bobby say he isn't smelly? What special powers do dogs have?

Chapter 2

Why isn't Mr Maskell's dog Bobby's special friend? Have the children support their views with evidence from the text. How does Bobby show he doesn't want Davy Dog near him?

Chapter 3

What does Bobby do to protect himself from dogs? How does Kevin scare Bobby? Why does he do this?

Chapter 4

Why does Charlie worry about Kevin Joggs? How does the author show that Charlie regrets beating him up? How does dad give Charlie an idea? What does Charlie to do to make Bobby feel less scared of the guard dog? How has Bobby changed? Ask the children to refer back to the text when answering these questions.

9

Response to text

Chapter 1

Ask the children if they think Charlie's family like football too much. Why? Why not? How do the children feel about football? Why do they feel like that?

Chapter 2

Were the children surprised by Davy Dog's behaviour? Why? Why not? Do they think Davy's behaviour is funny or naughty? Why do they think this? Are they surprised by Bobby's reaction to Davy? How would they have reacted to the puppy's behaviour?

Chapter 3

Do the children sympathise with Bobby's reaction to the poodle? Why? Why not?
Do they think the poodle's owner should have been more thoughtful?

Chapter 4

Kevin is a bully. Charlie says she beat him up when he tried to bully Bobby. Does this make Charlie a bigger bully than Kevin? Have the children give reasons to support their answer.

Next steps

Children read on in the book, keeping a record of descriptive language and similes on CM1. Encourage them to say why the author has used these words and phrases. Suggest children work in pairs to complete their lists. Children begin to use CM2 to map the main events in the stories.

Session 2 (AF2, AF3, AF6)

Introduction

Remind the children of the questions posed in the blurb. Ask them to predict how the author will answer those questions in the rest of the story. Have them suggest ways in which the questions may be resolved. List their solutions on the whiteboard.

Strategy check

Tell the children you want them to keep in mind their predictions as to what will happen in the narrative and to be prepared to revise their predictions in the light of the evidence they find in the text.

9

Independent reading

Have the children read the rest of the story noting how the narrative unfolds and how the author resolves the issues of Bobby's fear of dogs and Kevin's bullying.

Return to the text

Chapter 5

> Ask the children to give examples from the text of how Bobby has changed.

Chapter 6

> Why does Charlie need Bobby's help? What do Mum and Dad do to try and draw Bobby out of his shell? How successful are their strategies? Why is this?

Chapter 7

> How does Charlie persuade Bobby to come to the match with her? How does the author show that both Charlie and Bobby are nervous? Why does Charlie play so badly?

Chapter 8

> Why does Charlie feel she let Dad down with the way she behaved with Kevin?
> How does the author imbue Kevin's presence in the park with a sense of menace? Why doesn't Charlie leave the pitch to help Mr Maskell? What happened when Charlie scored?

Chapter 9

> How does the author show that Kevin is a very unpleasant person? What prevents Charlie from stopping Kevin tormenting Mr Maskell? How do Bobby and Davy stop Kevin from bullying Mr Maskell? What evidence is there in the text that shows us Bobby is a really brave person? Why is Davy a changed dog? Why does Bobby grin from ear to ear?

Response to text

Chapter 5

> Ask the children why they think Bobby has changed.

Chapter 6

> What else could Bobby's family have done to help him regain his confidence? Do the children think that Bobby is part of a loving family? Why? Why not?

Chapter 7

Why does Charlie want Bobby's support so much? Why is Charlie so nervous?

Ask the children if and when they have ever suffered from nerves and why?

Chapter 8

Ask the children how they feel about bullies like Kevin. What do they think Charlie should have done when Bobby called out to her? Was she right to carry on playing? Why? Why not? Do they think she really was unhappy when she scored the winning goal? Why? Why not? How would they have felt in her position?

Chapter 9

Ask the children what they think Mr Maskell must be feeling when Kevin torments him. Encourage them to give reasons to support their views. Ask the children to try and describe the thoughts that were going through Bobby's head when he saw what Kevin was doing to Mr Maskell. What do you think Charlie feels about her brother Bobby's actions? Why?

Next steps

Talk to the children about why Charlie does not get any pleasure from scoring the winning goal. How do they think the other players on both sides are feeling when the ball hits the back of the net? When you've discussed the issues ask the children to complete CM3.

Ask the children to tell you what a football commentator does. Explain that a commentator has to describe exactly what is happening on the pitch in a way that communicates the excitement and the drama of the game. Point out how a few well chosen adjectives and adverbs can really help bring a commentary to life, e.g. she scored an <u>incredible</u> goal; she ran <u>gracefully</u> past the defender. Let them practise commentating on Charlie's winning goal and then, when they are happy with their commentaries, have them complete CM4.

Writing opportunities

- Write a player card for your favourite footballer.
- Write a fact file on a famous football club.
- Write a letter from Mr Maskell to the Dog Training School telling them what a great job they have done with Davy.
- Draw a picture of a footballer and label each part of his/her kit.

Name . . . . Date . . . .

FOOTBALL CRAZY

Some people are football fans. Some people hate football. Make a chart showing three reasons why some people love football and three reasons why some people hate football.

Three reasons why people love football	Three reasons why people hate football

9 Pup on the Pitch (2)

Name . . . . Date. . . . .

RED CARD FOR BULLIES

Kevin is a bully. Charlie had a fight with him to stop him bullying Bobby. This is not the way to deal with a bully. Make a list of three things you can do to stop bullying behaviour.

Three Top Tips to Stop a Bully
1
2
3

Name . . . . Date. . . . .

GOAL OF THE SEASON

Draw a picture of Charlie scoring the winning goal. Show thought bubbles coming out of her head and the heads of the other players showing what they are thinking. Remember Charlie thinks it is the worst goal ever.

The Winning Goal

Name . . . . Date. . . . .

MATCH OF THE DAY

Imagine you are a football commentator. Write a short commentary describing Charlie's winning goal. The words in the box below may help you.

> dribble, swerve, trick, dash, race, hit, kick, fast, pace, goalie, dive, bulge, net, smash, defender, wallop, mud, post, cheer, happy, sad, excited, boot

STORY SYNOPSIS

There are four separate Horrid Henry stories in this book: Horrid Henry Eats a Vegetable; Horrid Henry's Underpants; Horrid Henry's Sick Day; Horrid Henry's Thank You Letter. The stories feature Horrid Henry doing what he does best: being a loveable anti-hero continually battling to outwit his annoyingly perfect brother Peter, his long-suffering parents and his teacher Miss Battle-Axe.

In Horrid Henry Eats a Vegetable, Henry tricks his parents into thinking he is eating his vegetables. They take him out to Gobble and Go, his favourite fast food restaurant, as a reward but Gobble and Go has gone.

In Horrid Henry's Underpants, Henry's great aunt sends him a pair of pink lacy pants. Henry inadvertently wears them to school. He spends the day trying to get rid of the pants and not get de-bagged. Unfortunately Miss Battle-Axe finds the pants and forces Henry to wear them for P.E.

In Horrid Henry's Sick Day, Henry is determined not to be outdone in the sickness stakes by Perfect Peter so he fakes an illness. Unfortunately it all backfires when both Dad and Mum are also taken ill and expect Henry to look after them.

In the final story, Horrid Henry's Thank You Letter, Henry has a brilliant money making idea – he will write thank you letters for his friends. However, Henry's thank you letters manage to upset everyone.

Chapter Synopsis
Horrid Henry Eats a Vegetable (p1-19)

Henry detests vegetables. He thinks they are absolutely disgusting. His brother, Perfect Peter adores them, as do his Mum and Dad. Henry's idea of a proper vegetable is tomato ketchup. His Mum makes a deal with him that if he eats all his vegetables for five days, the family will all go to Henry's favourite fast food restaurant Gobble and Go. Henry agrees but has no intention of actually eating his vegetables. He pulls off a number of ruses such as hiding his peas under his knife and hiding sprouts in a drawer and thereby convinces his parents he has kept his side of the bargain. However, all Henry's trickery is in vain because when the family arrive at the restaurant they discover Gobble and Go is no more. It is now The Virtuous Veggie.

Horrid Henry's Underpants (p21-41)

Henry receives a late birthday present from his Great-Aunt Greta. He hopes it will be money but it turns out to be a pair of frilly lace pink pants. Great-Aunt Greta thinks Henry is a girl. Henry is furious and hides them at the back of his pants drawer. One morning he oversleeps and has to get dressed for school in a hurry. He accidentally puts on the pink pants. The latest craze at school is for de-bagging and Henry spends the day in fear they someone will see them. He tries to make Perfect Peter swap pants but Peter won't. Henry hides the pants in the boys' toilets. Henry thinks he is safe but he has forgotten that the last lesson is PE. He tells Miss Battle-Axe that he has forgotten to wear pants so he can't do PE. Miss Battle-Axe tells Henry it's his lucky day. She has found the pink ones and she expects Henry to wear them.

Horrid Henry's Sick Day (p43-61)

Perfect Peter is ill. Mum lets him stay at home and miss school. Henry wants to stay at home too so he fakes an illness. He is allowed to stay at home. Mum and Dad argue about who is going to look after the boys. Mum loses and Dad goes off to work. Henry and Peter squabble over which TV programme they are going to watch. Mum takes their temperatures. Then Peter wants to be sick. While Mum and Peter are out of the room, Henry puts Peter's thermometer in a glass of cold water and puts his own next to the light bulb. He wants to show Mum he is sicker than Peter. Mum is very suspicious of the results. Henry says the thermometers must be broken. Dad comes home. He is unwell. Mum has to look after them all. This makes her ill. When it is too late to go to school, Henry decides he is better. He thinks he is going to have fun watching TV but his family insist he look after them. Henry goes back to his sick bed.

Horrid Henry's Thank You Letter (p62-81)

Mum wants Henry to write his Christmas thank you letters. Henry hates writing thank you letters. Mum tells him he can't watch any more TV until he does. Dad tells Henry he has to write one page for each letter so Henry uses gigantic handwriting. This makes Mum cross and she tells him he must write five sentences. Henry does so but he doesn't write nice sentences. He has written a no thank you letter which he sends to his Aunt Greta and Aunt Ruby. Then Henry has a brainwave. Everyone he knows hates writing thank you letters so he thinks he will make lots of money by writing thank you letters for his friends. The children at school all give him money to write their letters for them.

Unfortunately, Henry is so lazy that he uses his computer to write one very impersonal thank you/no thank you letter. He sends a copy of it to everyone. Naturally, they are all upset when they receive it. Henry can't understand why they are all making such a fuss but then his Aunt Ruby phones Henry's Mum to complain about the no thank you letter Henry sent her. Henry's get-rich-quick scheme has landed him in big trouble.

GUIDED READING – HORRID HENRY'S UNDERPANTS

APP Reading Links

Assessment Focus
AF1 - Session 1: Level 3
AF2 - Session 1: Level 3
        Session 2: Level 3
AF3 - Session 1: Level 3
        Session 2: Level 3
AF6 - Session 1: Level 3
        Session 2: Level 3

Session 1 (AF1, AF2, AF3, AF6)

Book introduction
Encourage the children to look carefully at the front and back covers of the book. Ask them to see how many clues they can find that show what kind of a character Henry is. Tell the children that the boy on the back cover wearing the rabbit suit is Henry's brother, Peter. See if they can work out what kind of a character he is by the way the illustrator has drawn him.

Strategy check
Help the children to identify the main points about Henry and his family by reading up to the end of page 5. List these points on the board, e.g. Henry hates vegetables while his Mum, Dad and Peter love them. (p2). Now discuss how they think the author is going to use these character differences to develop the story.

Independent reading

Ask the children to read the rest of the story, "Horrid Henry Eats a Vegetable" and to think about how the author shows Henry outwitting his parents but ends the story with a plot twist that turns the tables on Henry.

Return to the text

Ask the children how Henry tries to convince his parents that he does eat vegetables (p2/3). How does the author show that Henry does not have a very healthy diet (p3)? Why is Gobble and Go Henry's favourite restaurant (p5)? What does Henry think his parents will say if he is poisoned by vegetables (p9)? How does Henry manage to get Peter to eat Henry's string beans (p12/13)? Ask the children why Dad says that Peter's not a baby anymore (p14)? Have them use evidence from the text to support their views. Why doesn't Henry flick sprouts at Peter's head (17)? Give examples from the text to show how the author uses slapstick humour to make the story funny.

Why is it impossible to miss Gobble and Go (p18)? How do we know that Henry is beaten (p19)?

Response to text

How do we know that Peter is a well behaved boy? Encourage the children to use words from the text to support their answers. Why does Henry agree to eat his vegetables? Ask the children if they think Henry is being reasonable when he says he hates vegetables. Are Henry's tricks funny or irritating? Why? Is the deal Mum makes with Henry fair? Why? Why not? Ask the children if they think Henry gets what he deserves at the end of the story. Have them give reasons for their response.

Next steps

Discuss the inventive ways in which Henry manages not to eat his vegetables. Now look at CM1 with the children. See if they can be just as inventive as Henry by thinking up a cunning plan not to eat carrots. When they have thought of a plan have them complete CM1.

Ask the children to map out the "Horrid Henry Eats a Vegetable" story in the correct sequence. They can use CM2 to do this.

Session 2 (AF2, AF3, AF6)

Introduction

Show the children the illustration on page 20. Ask them to describe what Henry is thinking about and if they think his thoughts may have something to do with the letter he is holding. Make a note of their responses on the white board.

Strategy check

Explain that skim reading is a very useful reading strategy as it allows you to find specific information quickly. For example, it can help them find out whether or not their ideas about the illustration are correct. Now show the children how to skim read by modelling reading pages 21-23 of the story "Horrid Henry's Underpants" rapidly looking for the reasons why Henry only wants money as a present and why Great-Aunt Greta has sent Henry such an inappropriate present. List those reasons and discuss whether or not the children sympathise with Henry.

Independent reading

Have the children read the rest of the story "Horrid Henry's Underpants". Encourage them to think about why Henry is so worried that people will discover that he is wearing girls' pants and what his attempts to make his brother swap pants with him tells us about Henry's character.

Return to the text

Ask the children to find evidence from the text that shows Henry doesn't want Ralph to see the pants (p24). How do we know that Henry doesn't like his brother (p24)? Why does Henry wear the pink pants to school (p26)? Why does Miss Battle-Axe tell William off (p27)? How does Henry make the class laugh (p28)? How does the author show that Henry only has himself to blame if the other children see his pants (p30)? Why were the blue pants in the Lost and Found no good to Henry (p32)? How does Henry try to trick Peter into swapping pants (p34/35)? What lesson has Henry forgotten about (p40)? What will Henry make Miss Battle-Axe do when he is king (p41)?

Response to text

Ask the children if they think Henry is right to be cross with Great-Aunt Greta? Why? Why not? How would they feel if you had been sent a present that was completely wrong for them? Why? Do the children think that Ralph and Henry really like each other?

Have them give reasons from the text to support their answers. What kind of a brother is Henry to Peter? Why do they think that? Would they like a brother like Henry? Why? Why not? Do they think Miss Battle-Axe was being fair when she insisted Henry wear the pink pants? Why do they think this? Do they feel sorry for Henry? Why? Why not?

Next steps

Have the children read Horrid Henry's Sick Day. When they have done so discuss with them what they think the story tells us about Henry as a person. For example, do they think he is clever and funny or selfish and lazy? When they have expressed their opinions ask them to complete CM3.

Ask the children to read the last story in the book, "Horrid Henry's Thank You Letter". Now have them use CM4 to write a short review of what happens in each story and say which one they like best and why.

Writing opportunities
- Use some of the rhymes in the text as models for writing own rhymes.
- Create a book of disguises for crocodiles.
- Write an alternative ending to the story.
- Write part of the story from the point of view of one of the other animals.
- Write a list of rules for good behaviour for the crocodile.
- Write part of the story as a play script.

Name . . . . Date . . . .

ONLY RABBITS EAT CARROTS

Henry came up with five brilliant ways not to eat string beans, broccoli, peas, cabbage and sprouts. Think up a fiendish plot that Horrid Henry can use to get out of eating carrots. Maybe he can secretly feed them to his pet rabbit?

Horrid Henry's Fiendish Plot Not To Eat Carrots

10 Horrid Henry's Underpants (2)

Name . . . . Date. . . . .

PANTS!

Make a story map for the "Horrid Henry's Underpants" story.
Make sure you get the events in the correct sequence. Use the box below to help you.

Characters

Setting

This story begins when

The problem is

The next thing that happens is

Then

After that

Finally

Name . . . . Date. . . . .

A BAD LAD

Horrid Henry is always thinking up fiendish plots. In Horrid Henry's Sick Day he pretends to be ill so he can stay at home and watch TV. Make a wanted poster that explains who he is, who wants him caught and why they want him caught.

For example, it could be Miss Battle-Axe who wants him caught and punished for pretending to be ill and missing a day of her horribly hard lessons.

WANTED
HORRID HENRY

Name . . . . Date . . . .

HORRID HENRY'S NOT HORRIBLE!

Write a short review of what happens in each of the Horrid Henry stories in this book and say which story you like best and why.

My Reviews of:

Horrid Henry Eats a Vegetable

Horrid Henry's Underpants

Horrid Henry's Sick Day

Horrid Henry's Thank You Letter

My favourite story is:

My favourite character is this story is:

I like this character because:

My least favourite character in this story is:

I don't like this character because:

I like this story best because:

ENJOY GUIDED READING
Key Stage 1: Level 2A>3
APP READING LINKS

For the novels:

- **Mark Spark in the Dark** by Jacqueline Wilson
- **Cool as a Cucumber** by Michael Morpurgo
- **The Finger Eater** by Dick King-Smith
- **Harry the Poisonous Centipede** by Lynn Reid Banks
- **The Pea and the Princess** by Mini Grey
- **Winnie's New Computer** by Korky Paul & Valerie Thomas
- **The Enormous Crocodile** by Roald Dahl
- **Dinosaur School** by Dick-King Smith
- **Pup on the Pitch** by Sophie Smiley
- **Horrid Henry's Underpants** by Francesca Simon

ENJOY GUIDED READING: KS1: Level 2A>3 APP READING LINKS

Assessment of reading is important if children are to make progress. The sessions planned are designed to allow for the teaching and assessment of specific assessment focuses for reading. The levels below refer to the APP assessment guidelines and will support teachers with addressing any gaps the children may have.

Assessment Focus	Level 2	Level 3
AF1 – use a range of strategies, including accurate decoding of text, to read for meaning	**In some reading** • range of key words read on sight • unfamiliar words decoded using appropriate strategies, *e.g. blending sounds*	**In most reading** • range of strategies used mostly effectively to read with fluency, understanding and expression
AF2 – understand, describe, select or retrieve information, events or ideas from texts and use quotation and reference to text	**In some reading** • some specific, straightforward information recalled, *e.g. names of characters, main ingredients* • generally clear idea of where to look for information, *e.g. about characters, topics*	**In most reading** • simple, most obvious points identified though there may also be some misunderstanding, *e.g. about information from different places in the text* • some comments or quotations from or references to text, but not always relevant, *e.g. often retelling or paraphrasing sections of the text rather than using it to support comment*
AF3 – deduce, infer or interpret information, events or ideas from texts	**In some reading** • simple, plausible inference about events and information, using evidence from text, *e.g. how a character is feeling, what makes a plant grow.* • comments based on textual cues, sometimes misunderstood	**In most reading** • straightforward inference based on a single point of reference, e.g. 'he was upset because it says he was crying'" • responses to text show meaning established at a literal level e.g. *"walking good means walking carefully"* or based on personal speculation *e.g. a response based on what they personally would be feeling rather than feelings of character in the text.*
AF4 – identify and comment on the structure and organisation of texts, including grammatical and presentational features at text level	**In some reading** • some awareness of use of features of organisation, *e.g. beginning and ending of story, types of punctuation*	**In most reading** • a few basic features of organisation at text level identified, with little or no linked comment, e.g. *'it tells about all the different things you can do at the zoo'*
AF5 – explain and comment on writers' use of language, including grammatical and literary features at word and sentence level	**In some reading** • some effective language choices noted e.g. *"slimy" is a good word there'* • some familiar patterns of language identified e.g. *once upon a time, first, next, last*	**In most reading** • a few basic features of writer's use of language identified, but with little or no comment e.g. *'there are lots of adjectives'* or *'he uses speech marks to show there are lots of people there'*
AF6 – identify and comment on writers' purposes and viewpoints, and the overall effect of the text on the reader	**In some reading** • some awareness that writers have viewpoints and purposes, e.g. *'it tells you how to do something'*, *'she thinks it's not fair'* • simple statements about likes and dislikes in reading, sometimes with reasons	**In most reading** • comments identify main purpose, e.g. *'the writer doesn't like violence'* • express personal response but with little awareness of writer's viewpoint or effect on reader, e.g. *'she was just horrible like my nan is sometimes'*
AF7 – relate texts to their social, cultural and historical traditions	**In some reading** • general features of a few text types identified e.g. *information books, stories, print media*	**In most reading** • some simple connections between texts identified e.g. *similarities in plot, or books by same author, about same characters* • recognition of some features of the context of texts e.g. *historical setting, social or cultural background*

ENJOY GUIDED READING: KS1: Level 2A>3 APP READING LINKS

Each title has two Guided Reading sessions based on the text. If the sessions are followed, as laid out in this book, the following assessment focuses will be addressed. S = Session

Assessment Focus	Mark Spark in the Dark	Cool as a Cucumber	The Finger Eater	Harry the Poisonous Centipede	The Pea and the Princess
AF1 – use a range of strategies, including accurate decoding of text, to read for meaning	S1: L2/3 S2: L2/3	S1: L2/3 S2: L2/3	S1: L2/3 S2: L2/3	S1: L2/3 S2: L3	S1: L3 S2: L2/3
AF2 – understand, describe, select or retrieve information, events or ideas from texts and use quotation and reference to text	S1: L2/3 S2: L2/3		S1: L2/3 S2: L2/3		
AF3 – deduce, infer or interpret information, events or ideas from texts	S1: L2/3 S2: L3	S1: L2/3 S2: L2/3	S1: L2 S3: L3	S1: L2 S2: L2/3	S1: L2/3 S2: L2/3
AF4 – identify and comment on the structure and organisation of texts, including grammatical and presentational features at text level	S2: L2/3		S2: L 2/3		
AF5 – explain and comment on writers' use of language, including grammatical and literary features at word and sentence level		S1: L2/3 S2: L2/3		S1: L2 S2: L3	S2: L2/3
AF6 – identify and comment on writers' purposes and viewpoints, and the overall effect of the text on the reader	S2: L2/3			S1: L2 S2: L3	S1: L2/3 S2: L2/3
AF7 – relate texts to their social, cultural and historical traditions			S1: L2/3 S2: L2/3		S1: L2/3 S2: L3

ENJOY GUIDED READING: KS1: Level 2A>3 APP READING LINKS

Each title has two Guided Reading sessions based on the text. If the sessions are followed, as laid out in this book, the following assessment focuses will be addressed. S = Session

Assessment Focus	Winnie's New Computer	The Enormous Crocodile	Dinosaur School	Pup on the Pitch	Horrid Henry's Underpants
AF1 – use a range of strategies, including accurate decoding of text, to read for meaning	S1: L1/2 S2:L3	S1: L2/3 S2: L2/3	S1: L2/3 S2: L3		S1: L3
AF2 – understand, describe, select or retrieve information, events or ideas from texts and use quotation and reference to text			S1: L3 S2: L3	S1: L3 S2: L3	S1: L3 S2: L3
AF3 – deduce, infer or interpret information, events or ideas from texts	S1: L2/3 S2: L3	S1: L2/3 S2: L3	S1: L2/3 S2: L3	S1: L3 S2: L3	S1: L3 S2: L3
AF4 – identify and comment on the structure and organisation of texts, including grammatical and presentational features at text level		S1: L2 S2: L2			
AF5 – explain and comment on writers' use of language, including grammatical and literary features at word and sentence level	S1: L2 S2: L3	S1: L2/3 S2: L2/3			
AF6 – identify and comment on writers' purposes and viewpoints, and the overall effect of the text on the reader	S1: L2/3 S2: L2/3	S1: L2 S2: L3	S1: L2/3 S2: L3	S1: L3 S2: L3	S1: L3 S2: L3
AF7 – relate texts to their social, cultural and historical traditions	S1: L2/3 S2: L3		S1: L3 S2: L3		

Enjoy Guided Reading! – *Fiction*

Guided Reading guidance on popular reading books and novels

KS1 Teacher Books *Julie Galliard*

Level 2C > 2B Teacher Book with Copymasters	ISBN 978 1 84926 496 9
Level 2C > 2B Teacher Book with Copymasters + CD	ISBN 978 1 84926 497 6
Level 2A Teacher Book with Copymasters	ISBN 978 1 84926 499 0
Level 2A Teacher Book with Copymasters + CD	ISBN 978 1 84926 500 3
Level 2A > 3 Teacher Book with Copymasters	ISBN 978 1 84926 502 7
Level 2A > 3 Teacher Book with Copymasters + CD	ISBN 978 1 84926 503 4

KS1 covers the following novels, available in packs of 6 from Badger Learning:

Level 2C > 2B

We're Going on a Lion Hunt	by David Axtell	ISBN 978 1 84691 016 6
The Pig in the Pond	by Martin Waddell	ISBN 978 1 84691 023 4
Mr Gumpy's Motor Car	by John Burningham	ISBN 978 1 84691 022 7
Peace at Last	by Jill Murphy	ISBN 978 1 84691 017 3
Mog at the Zoo	by Jan Pienkowski	ISBN 978 1 84691 019 7
Owl Babies	by Martin Waddell	ISBN 978 1 84691 024 1
Sausages	by Jessica Souhami	ISBN 978 1 84926 505 8
Elmer and the Stranger	by David McKee	ISBN 978 1 84691 018 0
Willy the Wizard	by Anthony Browne	ISBN 978 1 84691 021 0
Princess Smartypants	by Babette Cole	ISBN 978 1 84691 020 3

Level 2A

The Tunnel	by Anthony Brown	ISBN 978 1 84424 769 1
Room on the Broom	by Julia Donaldson	ISBN 978 1 84424 772 1
The Adventures of the Dish and the Spoon	by Mini Grey	ISBN 978 1 84926 506 5
The Leopard's Drum illustrated	by Jessica Souhami	ISBN 978 1 84424 776 9
My Friend Bear	by Jez Alborough	ISBN 978 1 84424 770 7
The Gruffalo	by Julia Donaldson	ISBN 978 1 84424 774 5
The Queen's Knickers	by Nicholas Allen	ISBN 978 1 84424 775 2
Dogger	by Shirley Hughes	ISBN 978 1 84926 507 2
The Emperor of Absurdia	by Chris Riddell	ISBN 978 1 84926 508 9
Scarface Claw	by Lynley Dodd	ISBN 978 1 84926 509 6

Level 2A > 3

Mark Spark in the Dark	by Jacqueline Wilson	ISBN 978 1 84424 761 5
Cool as a Cucumber	by Michael Morpurgo	ISBN 978 1 84424 763 9
The Finger-Eater	by Dick King-Smith	ISBN 978 1 84424 765 3
Harry the Poisonous Centipede	by Lynn Reid Banks	ISBN 978 1 84424 768 4
The Pea and the Princess	by Mini Grey	ISBN 978 1 84424 762 2
Winnie's New Computer	by Valerie Thomas	ISBN 978 1 84424 764 6
The Enormous Crocodile	by Roald Dahl	ISBN 978 1 84424 766 0
Dinosaur School	by Dick-King Smith	ISBN 978 1 84926 510 2
Pup on the Pitch	by Sophie Smiley	ISBN 978 1 84926 511 9
Horrid Henry's Underpants	by Francesca Simon	ISBN 978 1 84926 512 6

Enjoy Guided Reading, Fiction – Year 3

Year 3 **Book 1** Teacher Book with Copymasters   ISBN 978 1 84926 369 6
Year 3 **Book 1** Teacher Book with Copymasters + CD   ISBN 978 1 84926 370 2
Year 3 **Book 2** Teacher Book with Copymasters   ISBN 978 1 84926 372 6
Year 3 **Book 2** Teacher Book with Copymasters + CD   ISBN 978 1 84926 373 3
Year 3 **Book 3** Teacher Book with Copymasters   ISBN 978 1 84926 375 7
Year 3 **Book 3** Teacher Book with Copymasters + CD   ISBN 978 1 84926 376 4
Year 3 **Book 4** Teacher Book with Copymasters   ISBN 978 1 84926 378 8
Year 3 **Book 4** Teacher Book with Copymasters + CD   ISBN 978 1 84926 379 5

Year 3 covers the following novels, available in packs of 6 from Badger Learning:

Year 3, Book 1
Dear Greenpeace	by Simon James	ISBN 978 1 84424 441 6
The Magic Finger	by Roald Dahl	ISBN 978 1 84424 443 1
The Diary of a Killer Cat	by Anne Fine	ISBN 978 1 84424 444 3
Dragon Ride	by Helen Cresswell	ISBN 978 1 84424 445 7
Dinosaur Trouble	by Dick King-Smith	ISBN 978 1 84926 423 5
Horrid Henry and the Mega Mean Time Machine		
	by Francesca Simon	ISBN 978 1 84926 424 2

Year 3, Book 2
The Three Little Wolves and the Big Bad Pig by Eugene Triviazas &		
	Helen Oxenbury	ISBN 978 1 84424 695 3
The True Story of the 3 Little Pigs	by Jon Scieszka &	
	Lane Smith	ISBN 978 1 84424 694 6
George's Marvellous Medicine	by Roald Dahl	ISBN 978 1 84424 691 5
The Hodgeheg	by Dick King-Smith	ISBN 978 1 84424 692 2
The Julian Stories	by Ann Cameron	ISBN 978 1 84424 693 9
The Owl who was Afraid of the Dark	by Jill Tomlinson	ISBN 978 1 84926 426 6

Year 3, Book 3
Cinderboy	by Laurence Anholt	ISBN 978 1 84691 264 1
Sleepovers	by Jacqueline Wilson	ISBN 978 1 84691 265 8
Stanley and the Magic Lamp	by Jeff Brown	ISBN 978 1 84926 431 0
Lion at School	by Philippa Pearce	ISBN 978 1 84691 267 2
The Worst Child I Ever Had	by Anne Fine	ISBN 978 1 84691 268 9
The Minpins	by Roald Dahl	ISBN 978 1 84691 269 6

Year 3, Book 4
Jack Sweettooth	by Malorie Blackman	ISBN 978 1 84691 820 9
Jack Slater Monster Investigator	by John Dougherty	ISBN 978 1 84691 821 6
Stink and the Great Guinea Pig Express by Megan Mcdonald		ISBN 978 1 84691 822 3
Dirty Bertie: Fetch	by David Roberts	ISBN 978 1 84926 438 9
Esio Trot	by Roald Dahl	ISBN 978 1 84691 824 7
The Killer Cat Strikes Back	by Anne Fine	ISBN 978 1 84691 825 4

Enjoy Guided Reading, Fiction – Year 4

Year 4 Book 1 Teacher Book with Copymasters	ISBN 978 1 84926 381 8
Year 4 Book 1 Teacher Book with Copymasters + CD	ISBN 978 1 84926 382 5
Year 4 Book 2 Teacher Book with Copymasters	ISBN 978 1 84926 384 9
Year 4 Book 2 Teacher Book with Copymasters + CD	ISBN 978 1 84926 385 6
Year 4 Book 3 Teacher Book with Copymasters	ISBN 978 1 84926 387 0
Year 4 Book 3 Teacher Book with Copymasters + CD	ISBN 978 1 84926 388 7
Year 4 Book 4 Teacher Book with Copymasters	ISBN 978 1 84926 390 0
Year 4 Book 4 Teacher Book with Copymasters + CD	ISBN 978 1 84926 391 7

Year 4 covers the following novels, available in packs of 6 from Badger Learning:

Year 4, Book 1

The Owl Tree	by Jenny Nimmo	ISBN 978 1 84424 447 8
The Iron Man	by Ted Hughes	ISBN 978 1 84424 448 5
Bill's New Frock	by Anne Fine	ISBN 978 1 84424 449 2
Conker	by Michael Morpurgo	ISBN 978 1 84424 450 8
Freckle Juice	by Judy Blume	ISBN 978 1 84424 451 5
Blessu	by Dick King-Smith	ISBN 978 1 84424 514 7
Dumpling	by Dick King-Smith	ISBN 978 1 84424 515 4

Year 4, Book 2

James and the Giant Peach	by Roald Dahl	ISBN 978 1 84424 697 7
The Lion, the Witch and the Wardrobe by C.S. Lewis		ISBN 978 1 84424 698 4
The Worst Witch	by Jill Murphy	ISBN 978 1 84424 699 1
It's Too Frightening for Me	by Shirley Hughes	ISBN 978 1 84424 700 4
100 Mile an Hour Dog	by Jeremy Strong	ISBN 978 1 84926 427 3
The Enchanted Horse	by Magdalen Nabb	ISBN 978 1 84424 702 8

Year 4, Book 3

The Whistling Monster	by Jamila Gavin	ISBN 978 1 84926 432 7
The Amazing Story of Adolphus Tips by Michael Morpurgo		ISBN 978 1 84691 271 9
Man of the Match	by Sophie Smiley	ISBN 978 1 84691 272 6
Billy Bonkers	by Giles Andreae	ISBN 978 1 84691 273 3
Hacker	by Malorie Blackman	ISBN 978 1 84691 274 0
Smasher	by Dick King-Smith	ISBN 978 1 84691 275 7

Year 4, Book 4

Fantastic Mr Fox	by Roald Dahl	ISBN 978 1 84691 826 1
The Invisible Dog	by Dick King-Smith	ISBN 978 1 84691 827 8
Return of the 100 Mile an Hour Dog by Jeremy Strong		ISBN 978 1 84691 828 5
Dominic's Discovery	by Gervase Phinn	ISBN 978 1 84691 829 2
Toms Sausage Lion	by Michael Morpurgo	ISBN 978 1 84926 439 6
Pippi Longstocking	by Astrid Lindgren	ISBN 978 1 84691 831 5

Enjoy Guided Reading, Fiction – Year 5

Year 5 Book 1 Teacher Book with Copymasters	ISBN 978 1 84926 393 1
Year 5 Book 1 Teacher Book with Copymasters + CD	ISBN 978 1 84926 394 8
Year 5 Book 2 Teacher Book with Copymasters	ISBN 978 1 84926 396 2
Year 5 Book 2 Teacher Book with Copymasters + CD	ISBN 978 1 84926 397 9
Year 5 Book 3 Teacher Book with Copymasters	ISBN 978 1 84926 399 3
Year 5 Book 3 Teacher Book with Copymasters + CD	ISBN 978 1 84926 400 6
Year 5 Book 4 Teacher Book with Copymasters	ISBN 978 1 84926 402 0
Year 5 Book 4 Teacher Book with Copymasters + CD	ISBN 978 1 84926 403 7

Year 5 covers the following novels, available in packs of 6 from Badger Learning:

Year 5, Book 1

The Mousehole Cat	by Antonia Barber	ISBN 978 1 84424 456 0
The Stinky Cheese Man	by Jon Scieszka	ISBN 978 1 84424 457 7
Stig of the Dump	by Clive King	ISBN 978 1 84424 453 9
Street Child	by Berlie Doherty	ISBN 978 1 84424 454 6
Butterfly Lion	by Michael Morpurgo	ISBN 978 1 84424 455 3
Aquila	by Andrew Norriss	ISBN 978 1 84424 458 4

Year 5, Book 2

World According to Humphrey	by Betty G. Birney	ISBN 978 1 84926 428 0
Charlotte's Web	by E.B. White	ISBN 978 1 84424 703 5
Goodnight Mister Tom	by Michelle Magorian	ISBN 978 1 84424 704 2
The Illustrated Mum	by Jacqueline Wilson	ISBN 978 1 84424 705 9
How the Whale Became and other stories	by Ted Hughes	ISBN 978 1 84424 707 3
The Firework-Maker's Daughter	by Phillip Pullman	ISBN 978 1 84926 429 7

Year 5, Book 3

How to Be a Pirate	by Cressida Cowell	ISBN 978 1 84691 276 4
How to Train Your Dragon	by Cressida Cowell	ISBN 978 1 84691 277 1
Spy Dog	by Andrew Cope	ISBN 978 1 84691 823 0
Sleeping Sword	by Michael Morpurgo	ISBN 978 1 84926 433 4
ParentSwap	by Terence Blacker	ISBN 978 1 84691 280 1
The Queen's Nose	by Dick-King Smith	ISBN 978 1 84926 434 1

Year 5, Book 4

The Water Horse	by Dick King-Smith	ISBN 978 1 84691 837 7
A Dog So Small	by Philippa Pearce	ISBN 978 1 84691 834 6
The Time Traveling Cat	by Julia Jarman	ISBN 978 1 84691 833 9
Half Moon Investigations	by Eoin Colfer	ISBN 978 1 84691 832 2
The Diamond of Drury lane	by Julia Golding	ISBN 978 1 84691 836 0
Victory	by Susan Cooper	ISBN 978 1 84691 835 3

Enjoy Guided Reading, Fiction – Year 6

Year 6 Book 1 Teacher Book with Copymasters	ISBN 978 1 84926 405 1
Year 6 Book 1 Teacher Book with Copymasters + CD	ISBN 978 1 84926 406 8
Year 6 Book 2 Teacher Book with Copymasters	ISBN 978 1 84926 408 2
Year 6 Book 2 Teacher Book with Copymasters CD	ISBN 978 1 84926 409 9
Year 6 Book 3 Teacher Book with Copymasters	ISBN 978 1 84926 411 2
Year 6 Book 3 Teacher Book with Copymasters + CD	ISBN 978 1 84926 412 9
Year 6 Book 4 Teacher Book with Copymasters	ISBN 978 1 84926 414 3
Year 6 Book 4 Teacher Book with Copymasters + CD	ISBN 978 1 84926 415 0

Year 6 covers the following novels, available in packs of 6 from Badger Learning:

Year 6, Book 1
The Wizard of Oz	by L Frank Baum	ISBN 978 1 84926 425 9
Carrie's War	by Nina Bawden	ISBN 978 1 84424 459 1
Tom's Midnight Garden	by Phillippa Pearce	ISBN 978 1 84424 460 7
The Wreck of the Zanzibar	by Michael Morpurgo	ISBN 978 1 84424 461 4
Over Sea, Under Stone	by Susan Cooper	ISBN 978 1 84424 462 1
The Lottie Project	by Jacqueline Wilson	ISBN 978 1 84424 464 5

Year 6, Book 2
Bad Girls	by Jacqueline Wilson	ISBN 978 1 84424 709 7
The Indian in the Cupboard	by Lynne Reid Banks	ISBN 978 1 84424 710 3
The Blurred Man	by Anthony Horowitz	ISBN 978 1 84424 711 0
Tales from India retold	by J.E.B. Gray	ISBN 978 1 84424 712 7
The Railway Children	by E. Nesbit	ISBN 978 1 84424 713 4
The Secret Garden	by Frances Hodgson Burnett	ISBN 978 1 84924 714 1

Year 6, Book 3
Marley: A Dog like no other	by John Grogan	ISBN 978 1 84926 435 8
Groosham Grange	by Anthony Horowitz	ISBN 978 1 84691 283 2
Out of the Ashes	by Michael Morpurgo	ISBN 978 1 84691 284 9
Hitler's Canary	by Sandi Toksvig	ISBN 978 1 84691 285 6
Animals of Farthing Wood	by Colin Dann	ISBN 978 1 84926 436 5
Swallows and Amazons	by Arthur Ransome	ISBN 978 1 84926 437 2

Year 6, Book 4
Matilda	by Roald Dahl	ISBN 978 1 84926 440 2
The Portal	by Andrew Norriss	ISBN 978 1 84691 839 1
Running on the Cracks	by Julia Donaldson	ISBN 978 1 84691 840 7
Hetty Feather	by Jacqueline Wilson	ISBN 978 1 84926 441 9
The Peppermint Pig	by Nina Bawden	ISBN 978 1 84691 842 1
Framed	by Frank Cottrell Boyce	ISBN 978 1 84926 442 6

Enjoy Guided Reading, Fiction –
Gifted & Talented

Guided reading guidance on popular novels to stretch readers in Years 3-6

Teacher Book with Copymasters   ISBN 978 1 84691 252 8

Covering the following novels, available in packs of 6 from Badger Learning:

Measle and the Mallockee	by Ian Ogilvy	ISBN 978 1 84691 289 4
Tiger, Tiger	by Lynne Reid Banks	ISBN 978 1 84691 290 0
I Was a Rat!	by Philip Pullman	ISBN 978 1 84691 291 7
The Star of Kazan	by Eva Ibbotson	ISBN 978 1 84691 292 4
The Scarecrow and his Servant	by Philip Pullman	ISBN 978 1 84691 293 1

Enjoy Picture Books at Key Stage 2

Ideas and resources to support teachers and pupils to engage with picture books

Julie Galliard & Mary Anne Wolpert

Teacher Book with Copymasters   ISBN 978 1 84691 187 3

Covering the following picture books, available from Badger Learning:

Belonging	by Jeannie Baker	ISBN 978 1 84691 214 6
Two Frogs	by Chris Wormell	ISBN 978 1 84691 215 3
Once Upon an Ordinary School Day	by Colin McNaughton & Satoshi Kitamura	ISBN 978 1 84691 216 0
Traction Man is here!	by Mini Grey	ISBN 978 1 84691 217 7
Dear Diary	by Sara Fanelli	ISBN 978 1 84691 218 4
Wolves	by Emily Gravett	ISBN 978 1 84691 219 1

Guided Reading Pack   ISBN 978 1 84691 213 9
containing one of each of the above picture books

Enjoy Guided Reading! *Non-Fiction*

Guided Reading guidance on book-banded non-fiction titles

EGR: NF Year 1 Teacher Book	**ISBN 978 1 84926 360 3**
EGR: NF Year 1 Teacher Book + CD	**ISBN 978 1 84926 363 4**
EGR: NF Year 2 Teacher Book	**ISBN 978 1 84926 361 0**
EGR: NF Year 2 Teacher Book + CD	**ISBN 978 1 84926 364 1**
EGR: NF Year 2 *Plus* Teacher Book	**ISBN 978 1 84926 362 7**
EGR: NF Year 2 *Plus* Teacher Book + CD	**ISBN 978 1 84926 365 8**

Covering the following novels, available in packs of 6 from Badger Learning:

EGR: NF Year 1 Teacher Book	**ISBN 978 1 84926 360 3**
EGR: NF Year 1 Teacher Book + CD	**ISBN 978 1 84926 363 4**

A Windy Day	by Robin Nelson	ISBN 978 1 84926 230 9
Friends	by Katy Pike	ISBN 978 1 84424 996 1
Flowers	by Charlotte Guillain	ISBN 978 1 84926 231 6
Seasons	by Katy Pike	ISBN 978 1 84424 995 4
The Moon	by Charlotte Guillain	ISBN 978 1 84926 232 3
Stormy Weather	by Katy Pike	ISBN 978 1 84926 236 1
Divali	by Denise M. Jordan	ISBN 978 1 84691 004 3
This is my Digger	by Chris Oxlade	ISBN 978 1 84926 233 0

EGR: NF Year 2 Teacher Book	**ISBN 978 1 84926 361 0**
EGR: NF Year 2 Teacher Book + CD	**ISBN 978 1 84926 364 1**

The Sun's Energy	by Katy Pike	ISBN 978 1 84926 241 5
Life Cycle of a Frog	by Angela Royston	ISBN 978 1 84926 247 7
Smelling and Tasting	by Claire Llewellyn	ISBN 978 1 84926 234 7
I know That! Weather	by Claire Llewellyn	ISBN 978 1 84926 237 8
Body Parts	by Bobbi Neate	ISBN 978 1 84691 071 5
Reduce, Rescue, Recycle Glass	by Alexandra Fix	ISBN 978 1 84926 235 4
Tractors and Farm Vehicles	by Jean Coppendale	ISBN 978 1 84926 238 5

EGR: NF Year 2 *Plus* Teacher book	**ISBN 978 1 84926 362 7**
EGR: NF Year 2 *Plus* Teacher Book + CD	**ISBN 978 1 84926 365 8**

Investigate: Settlements and Cities	by Neil Morris	ISBN 978 1 84926 243 9
Go Facts: Birds	by Paul McEvoy	ISBN 978 1 84926 244 6
The Great Fire	by Deborah Fox	ISBN 978 1 84691 062 3
Oxford First Science Dictionary	by Graham Peacock	ISBN 978 1 84691 069 2
Vegetables	by Lola Schaefer	ISBN 978 1 84926 239 2
At the Fire Station	by Ruth Thomson	ISBN 978 1 84926 240 8
Florence Nightingale	by Jane Shuter	ISBN 978 1 84691 068 5

Enjoy Guided Reading! – *First Flight*

Guided Reading on popular titles that have come from Badger's Full Flight and First Flight series.

First Flight – Teachers Book *Jane A C West*
ISBN 978 1 84926 492 1

First Flight – Teachers Book & CD *Jane A C West*
ISBN 978 1 84926 493 8

First Flight Level 1

The Phantom Striker	by Jonny Zucker	ISBN 978 1 84424 825 4
Pest Control	by Alison Hawes	ISBN 978 1 84424 826 1
Shark's Fin Island	by Jane A C West	ISBN 978 1 84424 850 6
Scary!	by David Orme	ISBN 978 1 84424 828 5

First Flight Level 2

Car Boot Genie	Jillian Powell	ISBN 978 1 84424 847 6
Monster Cards	Jonny Zucker	ISBN 978 1 84424 848 3
Shhh! My Family are Spies	Jane Langford	ISBN 978 1 84424 819 3
Ghost Dog Mystery	Celia Warren	ISBN 978 1 84424 827 8
Chip Boy	Jillian Powell	ISBN 978 1 84424 851 3
Sky Bikers	Tony Norman	ISBN 978 1 84424 852 0

Full Flight – Teachers Book *Jane A C West*
ISBN 978 1 84926 494 5

Full Flight – Teachers Book & CD *Jane A C West*
ISBN 978 1 84926 495 2

Full Flight Level 1

Abducted by an Alien	Jonny Zucker	ISBN 978 1 85880 309 8
Summer Trouble	Jonny Zucker	ISBN 978 1 85880 310 4
Sleepwalker	Jillian Powell	ISBN 978 1 85880 311 1
The Reactor	Jillian Powell	ISBN 978 1 85880 312 8
Starship Football	David Orme	ISBN 978 1 85880 313 5
Race of a Lifetime	Tony Norman	ISBN 978 1 85880 314 2

Full Flight Level 2

The Bombed House	Jonny Zucker	ISBN 978 1 85880 370 8
Gang of Fire	Jonny Zucker	ISBN 978 1 85880 372 2
Big Brother @ School	Jillian Powell	ISBN 978 1 85880 374 6
Rollercoaster	Jillian Powell	ISBN 978 1 85880 376 0

Badger Learning
Rollesby Road,
Hardwick Estate,
King's Lynn
PE30 4LS
Tel: 01553 769209
Fax: 01553 767646

Enjoy Guided Reading
Key Stage 1: Level 2A>3 Teacher Book with Copymasters
ISBN 978 1 84926 502 7

Enjoy Guided Reading
Key Stage 1: Level 2A>3 Teacher Book with Copymasters & CD
ISBN 978 1 84926 503 4

Published 2011
Text © Julie Galliard & Roger Hurn 2011

Complete work © Badger Learning 2011

Note: Due to the nature of the internet - It is vital that you check internet links before they are used in the class room.

Publisher: David Jamieson
Senior Editor: Danny Pearson
Designer: Adam Wilmott
Cover illustration: Juliet Breese

We would like to thank all of the publishers for the permissions to use their titles.

Attempts to contact all copyright holders have been made. If any omitted would care to contact Badger Learning, we will be happy to make appropriate arrangements.

Printed in the UK